THE
FIRE
SHE SET

Leigh Overton Boyd with
Emily Adams and Lisa Overton

ISBN 978-1-0980-1006-5 (paperback)
ISBN 978-1-0980-1007-2 (digital)

Christian Faith Publishing, Inc.
832 Park Avenue
Meadville, PA 16335
www.christianfaithpublishing.com

Printed in the United States of America

In memory of Nancy and Frank Overton

Arson, after all, is an artificial crime… A
large number of houses deserve to be burnt.
—H. G. Wells

CONTENTS

MAJOR CHARACTERS

Name	Description
Leigh Elyn Overton (Boyd)	First daughter of Frank and Nancy Overton, narrator and author
Leslie Overton (Les)	Second daughter, younger sister to Leigh
Lisa Overton	Third daughter, younger sister to Leigh, "person of interest" in arson fire
Lizbeth Overton (Liz)	Youngest daughter, sister to Leigh
Nancy Ruth Dunham Overton	Mother to Leigh and her sisters
Frank Tooker Overton	Father to Leigh and her sisters
Ellen Dunham	Nancy's mother (Leigh's maternal grandmother)
Barbara Jill Dunham Auburn (Jill)	Nancy's sister (Leigh's aunt)
Douglas Auburn	Jill's husband (Leigh's uncle)
Kimberly Auburn	Jill's daughter (Leigh's cousin)
John Rogge	Family friend, took in the Overton girls after the fire, realtor, former mayor of Brigantine
Betsy Rogge	Wife of John Rogge
Emma Walker	"Mutti," mother of Betsy Rogge
John DeHaan, PhD	Expert fire forensic investigator
Lt. Detective Chuck DeFebbo	Atlantic County (NJ) prosecutor

James Barber (Jimmy)	Former Brigantine city manager and former captain in charge of homicides for the Atlantic County Prosecutor's Office (ACPO)
Walter J. Buzby II	Fire investigator with the Atlantic County Prosecutor's Office
Detective Joseph Fields	Ventnor City police detective
Linda Cole	Wife of Maurie
Maurice Y. Cole Jr.	"Maurie," attorney, executor of Nancy and Frank's estate
Jessica Boyd	Daughter of Leigh
Andrew Boyd	Son of Leigh (February 15, 1988, to May 29, 2000)

2008

THE JOURNEY BEGINS

We're hoping that somebody out there has a good heart and will come forward. It's not a question of punishment or revenge for us. It's really a question of closure.

—Karthi Vadivelu

Waterview condos, present day

Before I was conscious of thought or fear, these words formed in my mind, *What has she done now?* I woke up choking. I tried to hold my breath but couldn't stop coughing. My legs swung over the edge of the bottom bunk, ready to run.

Mom didn't sleep well, and sometimes when her medication wore off in the middle of the night, she would haunt the rooms downstairs. Bleary eyed, half stuck in another place, she might start cooking and then wander off. She had set fire to pans, fallen asleep on the couch with a burning cigarette, and once placed a ceramic ashtray overflowing with cigarette butts into a carefully preheated oven. But this particular night, I heard Mom shouting into the telephone.

"Help me!" she shouted. "The whole house is on fire." She sounded completely awake.

Three stumbling steps into the hall were as far as I got, half-blind and dizzy. Flames were racing up the stairs, leaping up with long arms toward me, blocking the path to my parents. I was trapped. A wall of intense heat slapped me backward. Blackness squeezed my chest and sent me reeling into the bedroom. I became aware that my sister Liz was right behind me. Was she crying? The youngest of us four girls at twelve years old, Liz had taken a step closer to the stairs and was already burned on her hands and arms. I couldn't remember her panic outside of my own. I needed air. There was no air. Making my way over to the bedroom window, I frantically pushed out the screen and hung my head out, choking. Billowing smoke followed me, enveloping my head in its noxious funnel as it attempted its own escape. I swung a leg up onto the narrow windowsill and stuck both legs out. I looked down. The hard-packed ground and patchy grass below seemed very far away. I shut my eyes tight.

For most of my life, I'd been stuck there—a seventeen-year-old girl in her blue-flowered baby-doll pajamas, panic-stricken on the narrow windowsill, with her head immersed in that dense, gray cloud of smoke.

***

Forty years later, I was back at that window. I gazed up from the asphalt parking lot in the pounding rain and stared at a row of identical brick-and-clapboard town houses. We lived just outside Atlantic City, New Jersey. Our townhome sat on the corner. Long since rebuilt, the new town house was just another undistinguished unit—with two stories, aluminum windows, flat metal roof, and nothing wasted on appearances. It looked like the one to the left and the one to the right and all the others across a hard cement walkway. I noticed two small faces looking in my direction from the sliding glass doors that led to our den. Little more than toddlers, the boys stood peeking around the edge of the drapes. They were statue-still and weren't smiling. I felt a jolt of fear move through me. It never occurred to me that children would ever live here again, because on that fateful night long ago, the neighbors woke to the sound of our sliding glass doors exploding. Subconsciously, my hand jerked to wave these boys away from the window, which was about to detonate.

The rain was slanting down in sheets now, plastering hair to my face. I heard the windshield wipers of the rental car beating a steady rhythm behind me. Inside the car, my teenage daughter waited impatiently for this trip to be over. "Why do we have to be here?" she whined once again. I wanted her to know some of her family history, of my history. I wanted her to understand something more about me. But what?

A dark-haired woman draped in a sarong appeared in the den window beside the boys and placed her hand on the shoulder of the smallest. She stared at me too. I realized I must look crazy to her—an unfamiliar middle-aged woman, standing in a downpour, dripping wet and staring into her home. Abruptly, the mother turned away from the window and walked toward the kitchen which I knew was just a few steps away.

The town houses seemed smaller than I remembered, updated now with cheap vinyl siding running horizontal instead of the original vertical pattern that matched the roofline. Section 8 housing, I guessed. When my family moved into this brand-new development forty years ago, the excitement of living in a brand-new home with all-new gleaming white appliances masked any thoughts of low-class living.

I had so thoroughly insulated myself from the facts of my childhood that labels like *poor* seemed foreign—not part of *my* story. The Waterview townhomes had probably always been the huddled homes of clerks, restaurant workers, and young families just starting out or for some, finally settling into a life of limited expectations.

This was where I started my sophomore year of high school. There's the window my sisters used to sneak out of late at night. That was an exact replica of the metal roof that melted after someone splashed accelerant all around the den and up the stairs and onto our bedroom floors and then threw a match. Those were the bedroom windows my three sisters and I leapt from that night. We escaped; but our parents, Frank and Nancy Overton, never did. Neither did our beloved dog, Winnie.

And these were the walkways and town houses where rumors swirled that summer that one of my sisters started the fire that killed Mom and Dad. Lisa was fourteen then and already caught up in the kind of trouble that brought policemen to our door. When Dad needed us on our best behavior, a little calm, Lisa was sneaking off to meet boys and smoke pot, often with our sister Leslie in tow. Neighbors reported they heard boys goofing off in front of our place that night and tires squealing just before the flames erupted. Kids swore they heard Lisa talking to some boys about how to set a fire. Maybe one of those boys, smitten with my smart and charismatic sister, tossed the match. Maybe.

Even though the accelerant used in that hot, fast-burning fire created distinctive flow patterns and revealed a deeply charred floor, the arson and murder investigation was quickly forgotten by the adult powers. Being teenage girls, we didn't understand. So we sisters packed up the few surviving family papers along with our prejudices and rumors, buried our parents, dug up the heirloom flower bulb garden we had planted outside the kitchen window, and left 805 Burk Court.

I wondered if the woman and children who lived in the town house now were haunted by our family ghosts. Did they ever catch a glimpse of Mom wandering the halls at night in her handmade red velour bathrobe? Did they see Dad sitting in his blue plaid easy chair in the den, smoking his cherished pipe, watching the news on TV? Maybe they even caught sight of me, perched on that windowsill, with my head stuck in the thick gray cloud, choking.

Nancy and Frank Overton had certainly haunted me. After they died that hot June night in 1974, I'd longed for them for years with a grief that refused to let go. Holidays and family events—college graduations, weddings, the birth of their first grandchild—only intensified the painful fact that they'd never be there. I would imagine the smell of Chanel No. 5 perfume that my mother wore or hear her bold, infectious laugh coming from the next room. My father would be a half step behind her, smiling at something she said, his kind eyes shining behind the thick black-framed glasses he always wore. Mom and Dad's flaws diminished with each year that passed. My sisters and I rarely spoke of them.

With the rain drumming cold against my head, I squinted and found myself willing that teenage girl on the windowsill to open her eyes, look over her shoulder, and try to remember. Could she hear Mom and Dad moving? Were there any boys running away? I knew she needed to jump. She needed to clear the way and let Liz jump too. And yet, I wanted her to wait. I needed to know more. For the first time in my life, I really wanted to know what happened.

I got back in the car and shut the door. I sat there dripping wet in the driver's seat, still staring at the house. Jessica crossed her arms and said, "It's so ghetto, Mom. Let's go." Jessica was about to go off to college, so of course she knew better than I did about a lot of things. I was not ready to stop being her mom. I knew how intense that line could be, the line between the time when you belonged to your parents and then the time when you didn't.

I put the car in drive and drove east, away from the Waterview townhomes. Driving carefully through the tattered streets of Ventnor Heights, I crossed the Intracoastal Waterway at the Dorset Avenue Bridge. Now we're in the neighborhood of the old summer estates—manor houses of warm beige stone and mullioned glass windows, their yards thick with manicured hedges and gnarled old shade trees, remnants of bygone Atlantic City resort days. Jessica picked at a fingernail, unimpressed.

We turned north, crossing into Atlantic City driving parallel to the Boardwalk through a city I barely recognized. The carnival smells from the Boardwalk—hot grease, sweat, and sugar—no longer permeated these streets. It was a legitimate casino town now where oversized hotel towers of colored glass adorned the flat beach like cheap costume jewelry—shiny gold, sparkly blue glass, silver, and neon. We drove past Caesars Boardwalk Regency Hotel and Casino where I was crowned Miss Atlantic City 1980, but Jessica had heard that story before.

Crossing the tall bridge over a narrow inlet, we made our way onto the island of Brigantine. A little more than ten square miles of South Jersey beach town, I remembered Brigantine as equal parts magic and desolation. In the summer, Brigantine meant hot sun and childhood freedom. Station wagons from wealthier inland towns pulled up on our street regularly, belching out pale kids with their brightly colored buckets and towels, ready for the beach. Day trippers carried their lunches in shoeboxes back then, so we called them *shoobies*. We would poke fun at these summer visitors, the shoobies, separating ourselves with righteous pride since *we* were the locals.

Our house was fourth from the beach on 29th Street. All my sisters and I had to do was stroll down to the sand to find new friends, new toys, and, later, boys. At night through our open windows, laughter and songs around illicit beach fires mingled with the lapping waves to lull us to sleep.

In winter, our weathered old house afforded meager protection against the elements. Every blade of cold, damp wind forced its way inside. The chill whistled in around ill-fitting doors and through breaks in the siding, despite the old blankets and towels we shoved into the cracks where weather stripping should have been. No tourists visited in winter.

I drove past the Presbyterian Church, reminded of the members who helped support us during Mom's illnesses and absences. I pointed out the house where our lawyer neighbor lived—the one who hired a criminal defense attorney for Lisa and always had a pitcher of martinis in the freezer. Up ahead was the mayor's house where I went to live after the fire.

Driving down those familiar streets, I felt I was having a conversation with Brigantine itself. Or rather, I was finding new questions to ask. Suddenly, it became an interrogation. Did you, our well-connected neighbors, encourage the arson investigation or squash it? Did you know about my mom? I didn't remember any of you talking about her to me. How come the mayor and his wife—John and Betsy Rogge, whom we affectionately referred to as Aunt and Uncle—stopped talking about the arson investigation so soon? It seemed strange now that the adults lost interest in the arson before a year had even passed. Was there a secret they were keeping?

Before I reached the Rogges' house, I made a decision. I needed to know what happened to my parents that night, to all of us, but mostly to them. It's not fair that they had missed so much. It's not fair that no one had been held accountable. Words like *justice* and *responsibility* brightly underlined themselves in my head. Even if the evidence pointed to my sister, I thought we all had the right to resolution, to closure. I felt resolved, even brave, as I parked the car in the Rogge driveway.

Had I known then that my investigation would take eight years and force me to redefine who I was, I might not have started this journey. As a single mother and a self-employed real estate consultant, I was content to live in the present. I was afraid to be a modern-day Pandora, opening the box where the ghosts and bad memories would be unleashed. In spite of my fears, I found the courage to open that box and gathered the strength to shove that teenage girl in the blue-flowered baby-doll nightie off that window ledge.

1974

Evidence of Arson

There are only two mistakes one can
make along the road to truth: not
going all the way, and not starting.
—Buddha

Fire photo, 805 Burk Court, June 1974

A copy of the Overton Arson Investigation file from the Ventnor
City Police Department, sent to me in California by a sympathetic
lieutenant, accompanied me everywhere for more than a month

before I mustered the courage to read it. Even though the report was forty pages long, the young lieutenant warned me there wasn't much information in it. Still, the file never left my side those first weeks. It sat on the back seat of my car as I traveled to appointments with clients, or it waited unopened on the kitchen counter as I brewed my morning coffee.

Back in the summer of 1974, within a week or so of the fire, Betsy Rogge told my sisters and me that the Atlantic County Prosecutor's Office had called in a special investigator who found suspicious markings on the floors. There was evidence of arson both upstairs in the hallways and downstairs in the den, Aunt Betsy said.

Soon after that, my fourteen-year-old sister Lisa was represented by a criminal defense attorney and was administered a lie detector test, but we never heard any conclusions. There was only speculation and then silence. I stayed on with the Rogges and counted myself lucky. My sisters journeyed north to live with my mother's sister, Jill, and her husband, Doug. For forty years, we sisters didn't discuss the fire except in passing. We would refer to our lives as *before* and *after* without even mentioning the summer of 1974. The fact of the fire and Lisa's involvement always lay uneasy between us, but not out loud. I would never leave Lisa alone in my house, especially when my children were young. We never talked about *why*. Now, it occurred to me that the answers might be sitting on the back seat of my car or on the kitchen counter. Maybe I would find proof on the very first page.

By this point, Lisa was nearly fifty years old and raising two girls of her own. After her teenaged years of running away, abusing drugs and alcohol, and bouncing in and out of institutions, she cleaned herself up, served in the Navy, and later earned a master's degree in counseling. Lisa worked hard to change her life. I love her daughters; they're funny and smart. I played a little what-if game, looking at the file. What if my sister really was the arsonist and I was the only one who knew? What would I do with that knowledge?

But how could that possibly be? Lisa was a suspect, and then she was not. Nobody was. Surely if our case had been a bona fide arson, it wouldn't have just disappeared the way it did. The death of my parents transformed arson into murder. There is no statute of limitations on murder. I picked up the oversized manila envelope containing the file, but I put it down again, unread.

On a sunny Saturday morning in October, while sitting in my car waiting on a friend, I finally opened it. Before the little what-if game could take root, I read the top pages quickly. These were the autopsy reports. My father's body was found in a pugilistic position with second-degree burns over 60 percent of his body. I forced myself to continue without imagining what that looked like. The anterior and pleural surfaces of his lungs were congested and cherry-red in color. His chest was regular and his abdomen protuberant. Both coronary arteries showed moderate degree of atherosclerosis. His bronchial passages had a considerable quantity of black, sooty material mixes with frothy fluid.

Mom had been burned over 75 percent of her body. Her pupils were opaque. I refused to imagine this too. Her nasal passages contained a frothy, turbid, hemorrhagic fluid. Her tongue was protruding. I felt sick to my stomach and skipped ahead. I kept getting stuck on the errors. Mom was much taller than the stated height of 5′3″. I had photos to prove it. I remembered clearly that she was taking Antabuse, so there was no way that her blood alcohol level could have been 0.133. She would have been violently ill if she drank even a single beer. She and Dad had both explained this to me. I felt nauseated, and the clinical description of my parents' body fat was not helping. I turned the page.

"As the floor in the den was cleared, a burn pattern normally associated with, or the result of, flammable liquid being spilled or poured became visible on the floor."

There. I wasn't dreaming that memory, the damning pattern left by the fire. Under the oval braided rug in the den, fire had clung tightly to the floor, bonding to the wood and charring it deeply. The burn marks looked like a pool of liquid. Photos 1 and 2 clearly showed the liquid pour pattern; it was possible to see the sharp contrast between burned and unburned flooring, the report stated. The pattern continued out into the hallway. There were more liquid pour patterns in the living room, but not in the kitchen. Two longer "liquid run" patterns were found along the west wall of the living room, under a balcony that led to the hallway outside my parents' bedroom door. All this evidence was visible in the photographs, one report stated. I rifled through the forty pages of the file, but found no images.

Closing my eyes, I was back in our town house with its open floor plan and cheap attempt at modernism. The doors were hollow, and the interior walls were thin. Sliding glass doors in the living room had led to what should have been a deck, but there was nothing except an iron railing we used to climb over to get to a lawn shared by eight or ten other families.

The real selling point of the four-bedroom model at Waterview townhomes was the living room's two-story vaulted ceiling. Halfway up the soaring walls, a balcony extended around two sides, leading from my parents' bedroom to the other bedrooms on the second floor. The liquid was poured just under those balconies and burned very hot, the report said. Flames shot up and filled the space, sucking up available oxygen and burning the underside of the balcony all the way through. If Liz and I had gotten closer to our parents' bedroom door that night, we might have fallen through the balcony floor.

The liquid pour pattern showed up again on the landing at the top of the stairs, the report said. It flowed up to, and just inside of, the master bedroom. The hallway upstairs was covered with hot spots of the type usually associated with flammable liquid spills. Another distinctive pour pattern flowed into the back bedroom where Liz and I slept. The pattern dripped down the hall, splashed into the middle bedroom—empty but for a roll-top desk, an old trunk, and charred walls—and stopped short of the front bedroom where Lisa and Leslie slept.

In conclusion, the report stated the fire appeared to have multiple points of origin and a liquid accelerant was used to aid the spread of this fire on the first floor and up to the second. *It was clearly arson.* Accelerant was poured over the threshold of my bedroom, but not Lisa's.

I wasn't breathing as I stared at the names of the investigators who wrote this report. They suspected someone poured accelerant all around the living room, walked up the stairs, and splashed it into my parents' bedroom and then into mine. They knew someone did this, and yet they dropped their investigation. Didn't they care? A few feet from where my sister and I lay sleeping on our bunk beds, someone soaked the threshold with accelerant knowing that a match would be next. Did this person see Liz and I on our beds, sprawled on top of thin sheets on that hot summer night, murmuring or twitching in our sleep?

Before reading this report, I never thought that someone was actually trying to kill us that night. But the char patterns in the floor seemed to point right at the bunk beds where Liz and I innocently slept. A hot flash of anger came over me.

I saw the fire now as a living entity, greedily spreading under pyro-perfect conditions. Every window in our house was open that night, the report noted, including the sliding glass doors in the living room and den. There were firewalls between us and our neighbors on each side, creating a kind of chimney, and the walls of the den had been covered in cheap pressboard paneling my father installed. All that rich fuel waited for the match. When the spark came, the flames became uncaged beasts, bounding up the walls and stairs to devour us as we slept on our beds. Every door was open to invite the fire in.

No evidence samples were taken during the first walk-through of the fire scene, the report stated. No samples? The pour patterns weren't discovered until the floors were cleaned two weeks after the fire. By then, everything had been hidden under debris and water for a long time. The investigators also noted the liquid accelerant used probably wasn't very explosive and flammable liquids were "not unknown" in our household. I was still trying to figure out the meaning of this strange list of facts when I noticed two other documents: The first page revealed a piece of rug was submitted to the state crime lab for testing. The second page concluded that no "added flammable hydrocarbons" were found on the rug sample. These lab reports were dated early and mid-August 1974. So the rug sample—and there was no indication which rug was sampled—wasn't even sent to the lab for testing until six weeks after the fire. Having a degree in criminal justice, I knew just enough to groan in despair. Feeling frustrated, angry, and helpless, I put the report down.

I remembered being allowed into the house, briefly, after the fire. The front porch was burned away, and the wall outside around my parents' bedroom window was a black smear that resembled a screaming mouth. The metal roof just above their window had melted down into a V shape. The neighbors' walls remained standing; but everything in between was cracked, black, and sagging.

Most of our living room and den furniture had been carted off to the city dump. Daylight slanted crazily through charred holes in the walls and ceilings. I still smelled the chemicals—the oily gaseous plastic fumes that I remembered from the night of the fire—only now they were stale and mixing with the stench of brackish water. The toxic fumes coated the inside of my mouth and throat again, and I felt relief when we were turned away at the stairs because the second floor was unstable. Nothing looked like ours in that black mass of garbage. The family Bible that chronicled four hundred years of the Dunham family, Mom's ancestors—beginning in the early 1600s and all the way through to the inscription of our names in my mother's careful hand—was lost.

Oddly, the closet under the stairs was untouched. Inside were photo albums from our childhood, letters between my mother and my grandmother, scraps of baby blankets, our christening gowns, and Mom's wedding dress. There were metal cans with film rolls, filled with home movies of the time before we moved to Brigantine, before the trouble, before my parents forgot who they were.

1957–1964

The Early Years

For in the Old Kingdom, she was Somebody.
—Nancy R. Dunham

News clipping, May 14, 1937

When we were no taller than the back of her chair, my mother would gather us girls around her knees and on her lap and tell us a story. "Once upon a time," she would say, "there was a king and a queen, and they had a beautiful princess whom they loved very much. Then the princess grew up and found a prince of her own, and she was filled with love. The princess had so much love, and that love became you," Mom would say, pointing at me. "Still, the princess was filled with more love, and it became you," she continued, tickling Leslie or Lisa or Liz until we squealed and begged for more.

All of us were made from love, and we were royalty when we still lived in Fords in northern New Jersey. We knew everybody, it seemed, and everyone knew Mom. We lived with Mom's mother in a sturdy little house on one of the town's main streets. Parades marched past our front stoop in the summer, and the family gathered at Grandmom's house for every birthday and holiday. Mom's sister, Jill, lived with her husband, Doug, in a house they built in the back of Grandmom's; and they started having babies just after I was born.

On Saturday nights, Mom and Dad might have a party in the basement that was fixed up like a nightclub. Red leather barstools accented a polished wooden bar, a ping-pong table beckoned challengers, and a record player waited to play dance music. Above the quarry stone fireplace, a mounted deer head kept watch over the mantle. Mom painted a mural on the concrete walls depicting Bourbon Street in New Orleans, even though she had never been. Everyone said she was a talented artist.

Mom and Dad were a popular couple. Their friends would come over and drink cocktails and dance in short conga lines that snaked round the room. Sometimes, their friends came and drank beer and played card games for fun. On some nights, Mom drank too much, and Dad would put her to bed.

Occasionally on a Saturday night, Mom and Dad would go out driving with Jill and Doug, down to a pretty spot on the Raritan River in Perth Amboy. They would bring six packs of Pabst beer and drink, sitting in the car watching a few lights play on the dark water while the freighter ships served as an industrial backdrop. One such night, Dad and Uncle Doug swore a solemn oath by the pitch-black river that they would take care of one another's children, just in case anything should happen.

On Sundays after church, Grandmom would set out a late-afternoon supper in the dining room, using her white linen tablecloths and starched napkins, Limoges china, and polished silver. All of us girls were dressed in ruffles and bows and our shiny, patent leather Mary Jane shoes. We ate well-done roast beef with brown gravy, buttery mashed potatoes, Harvard beets from a can, and crescent rolls that popped out of a cardboard tube. After dinner, Grandmom served crème de menthe over shaved ice in her elegant crystal glasses. While the adults stayed at the table, we girls cleared the dishes and set to work cleaning the kitchen. I was in charge of washing because I was tall enough to reach the faucet if I stood on a box. Always careful with Grandmom's china, I would wash and rinse, while the little girls dried and stacked the clean dishes on a table. Cleaning up took hours, until it was almost our bedtime, and we were all hungry again.

Mom was beautiful by anyone's standards, with her high cheekbones, wide-set hazel eyes, and toothy smile. Her hair was full and dark, set off by pale skin. She looked like a fairy book princess to me, and that was how she always described herself. But mostly, I think, everyone loved Mom for that mischievous look in her eye, like she knew what kind of fun was just about to break out.

From the beginning, Nancy Ruth Dunham was the center of attention. When Mom was just three-and-a-half years old, her father built her an elaborate playhouse in the backyard. The local newspaper ran a story on May 14, 1937, headlined, "This Playhouse Makes Dunham Girl 'Queen of the Neighborhood.'" It even had electricity. Nancy had heaps of friends; and later, when she attended the University of Connecticut (UConn), she was a princess in the court of the Football Hop Queen.

After only two years in college, where she majored in art and psychology, but suffering from homesickness, Nancy returned home to Fords. She had plenty of boyfriends, and some were quite handsome. In 1953, she married my father, Frank Tooker Overton, at Simpson Methodist Church with a simple reception afterward in the nightclub basement. They moved in with Grandmom soon after the honeymoon.

One after the other, we were born, four girls in five years—Leigh, Leslie, Lisa, and Liz. We were all bestowed with the initials L. E. O., so Grandmom could knit us personalized sweaters that we handed down. For several years, we named every family dog Leo too.

Mom wasn't a morning person, but it didn't matter. Grandmom was wholeheartedly devoted to us. She awoke every morning at five to get to her nursing job at Rahway State Prison. She set out graham crackers or cold cereal and milk and juice in the kitchen before she left for work. Mom made us lunch on the days we weren't in school—mostly peanut butter and marshmallow fluff sandwiches or Welsh rarebit that we loved so much we could eat it by the bucketful. Before sending us outside to play, she gathered us up and told us the story of the princess and the love that made little girls. Other times, she would tell us that being fat was a choice and we didn't have to be fat like Dad's sisters. We had a choice. Or she talked about the evils of smoking. She would say, "Be smart. Don't start," even though she and everyone else, it seemed, had a cigarette burning at all times.

In the daytime, Mom wore pedal pushers and button-up blouses or dungarees and one of Dad's flannel shirts. Before Dad got home, though, she put on a simple shirtdress or a bouncy, full skirt, her favorite gold hoop earrings, and Chanel No. 5. I can still see her coral lipstick staining the rim of a cocktail glass, from which we would steal sips when she wasn't looking.

For every Christmas and Easter holiday, Mom sewed us new dresses and decorated the house like Martha Stewart. Seasonal touches were added using fresh flowers and flora gathered from the garden or local woods. For Valentine's Day, she hung a big red paper heart decorated with doilies in the window; for Easter, there were pastel-colored baskets, white gloves, and hats with ribbons. The night before a big holiday event, I would sit perfectly still while she wrapped locks of my hair around her finger and jammed bobby pins into my head so that I too would be a princess. It hurt, but I didn't complain because Mom was paying attention only to me.

Mom baked elaborate cakes and planned themed parties for every birthday. One year, she staged a taffy pull for my birthday in March. The recipe was for molasses taffy, which was brown and tasted terrible, but it was a big success. At night, if it was snowing, she might take us to Roosevelt Park armed with a thermos of hot, steaming cocoa. She taught us to ice-skate, played with us in the snow and made snow angels, and took us tramping through the woods in search of pine cones, laurel branches, Winter Red holly berries, and pine boughs to decorate the house for Christmas. After Mom's sister, Jill, went back to work, Mom took care of Jill's daughter Kim during the day too, so there were usually five little kids trailing along after her. When the leaves turned color in autumn, Mom would help us collect the pretty ones off the ground and press them between two sheets of wax paper, sealing them with a hot iron to make placemats for our kitchen table.

We were always busy. When Mom was doing laundry, cleaning the house, or working on a special sewing project, Dad taught us to build a go-cart and raced it with us down 3rd Street. Three of us could pile into the cart. I can still see the asphalt coming at us fast and hard as we clattered down the street, wind in our faces going much too fast until we tumbled over in a wheel of bloody knees and tears, and that ended that.

Mom enrolled us in Miss Luba's dance classes so we could become graceful and coordinated, but my skinned knees and awkward poses were proof that I was hopeless. On my first day of second grade, though, Mom showed me how to push the sleeves of my sweater up to my elbow because that's what big girls did. By her smile, I knew I'd gotten one thing right.

That was me—the big girl, always trying to please. "Take your sisters outside to play," Mom would say. "Help your sister find her shoes. Set a good example."

To my sisters, I was bossy. If they didn't listen to me, I would pull their arms or pinch them. They didn't understand how important it was to behave. Sometimes, it felt like I was the only one who could see a bad thing coming, who had a sense of dread, like the one Sunday we were all scrambling to get in the car and go to a rare family party at someone else's house. All of us girls were wearing dresses that had to stay clean. Lisa's socks were supposed to match. Nobody remembered to dress Liz until the last minute. Leslie's hair was a fright. Grandmom had already gone ahead to the party.

I do remember all of us girls finally piling into the back seat of the wood-sided station wagon and seeing my mom at the front door, calling to the dog. We always had a dog, usually named Leo, but this little brown dog we named Lizzie. She looked like a sweet mix of Labrador and Golden Retriever and was still a clumsy pup. Mom said Lizzie could trip over her own paws.

Dad was already in the front seat, smoking a cigar and complaining. "Always late," he was muttering. "Why do we always have to be late?" Mom yelled for Lizzie again and Leslie said "Hey!" as Lisa slid fast and hard across the bench seat and pushed Leslie into the crack between the door and the seat.

Dad honked the horn, even though Mom was right there. She frowned. Lisa laughed until Leslie slapped her. I lunged over Liz to grab at Lisa, but only caught a piece of her sleeve. Suddenly Mom was at the window. "Why am I the only one trying to get the dog in the yard?" she fumed at Dad.

"We're late. Get in the car."

Mom went around to the passenger side and then suddenly knelt down, and I could hear her through the open window saying, "There you are. C'mon, Lizzie. Out."

Dad sighed and twisted the key in the dashboard. The engine coughed and then roared. I could smell the oily smoke pushing back up the driveway as Mom got in the car. Lisa pushed at my hand and hissed, "Stop pinching me. I'll tell." I pulled my hand away and glared at her instead.

"Frank, Lizzie is still under the car."

"She'll run out when we start moving."

Mom slammed her door shut and crossed her arms. "We're not late. The girls and I have to look nice, unlike you."

I felt sick to my stomach as Dad lowered the emergency brake and the car rolled backward. Mom's hand shot out and grabbed Dad's arm. "Frank!" she screamed. But we all heard the sharp yelp, the sickening soft crunch under the wheels, and then the silence. The car jerked to a halt.

Mom yelled, opened her door, jumped out, and ran around the car. She ripped open my door and told us, "Get out right now; go into the house, and don't look back!" I had to yell at Lisa and Leslie to get away from the living room windows. We all sat on the carpeted floor and cried.

Mom got another dog the very next day. She named him Leo and said we shouldn't think about Lizzie. The thing that happened to Lizzie was sad, but it was done, and there was no sense crying over spilled milk.

1965

BRIGANTINE

Childhood is a short season.

—Helen Hayes

Leslie, Liz, Leigh, and Lisa, circa 1962

In the summer of 1965, I was eight years old. Dad graduated from Seton Hall and earned his first tenured job of his new career, teaching sixth grade at Massachusetts Avenue Elementary School in Atlantic City, one hundred miles south on the Garden State Parkway. Mom told us it would be an exciting new adventure and we would live close to the beach. The whole plan sounded pretty dubious especially since it didn't include Grandmom, a very bad omen. I had a sense of dread from the moment I first heard the news. My worries stayed with me. Just before moving day, while riding my bike to my best friend's, John Lefkowicz, house to say goodbye, I got hit by a car. I ended up in the hospital with a concussion and thirty-two stitches in my left knee. Mom was angry with me since she was in the middle of packing up the house and her life into brown cardboard boxes. Dad had already headed south so he wouldn't miss the first day of school. As soon as they released me from the hospital, Mom, my sisters, and I followed him to Brigantine. Nothing was going to stand in the way of this move; Mom and Dad were determined to start their new lives.

The house at 29th Street and Ocean Avenue stood on a corner lot, one of the best locations on Brigantine, even if the house itself was neglected and weather worn. Aunt Betsy told me once that Uncle John as our realtor tried to direct my parents to a nearby house, mid-block, that was several thousand dollars cheaper and in better repair but Mom would have none of it. Aunt Betsy said that if you gave Mom a nickel, she would spend a dime.

The house was a simple, faded two-story Cape Cod with clapboards once painted white, scrubbed to a mottled gray by the wind from the ocean. The upstairs wooden deck was in danger of separating from the house, so we weren't allowed to play there. Still, this was our family's first real house on our own, and Mom was determined to make it fun.

In the kitchen, Mom covered the bottom half of the walls with contact paper that looked like corkboard and helped us hang our school art projects there. Above that, she painted the walls white and offered visitors a big black marker to leave graffiti notes about their stay. A rough wooden picnic table with bench seats served as the table where we ate all our meals and did our school homework. Both family and guests were encouraged to carve their names into it; and I remember sitting there for hours on end, struggling with math, picking at suppers that would last forever, idly tracing the grooves in the wood.

In the utility room, near the back door, Dad built serviceable shelves for a pantry; and that's where we kept the big red and white box of Carnation instant milk. It was often my job to make the milk, mixing powder with water in a half-gallon plastic pitcher. The powder was creamy white as it came spilling out of the box but turned faintly blue when it hit the water, thin and fake, a shadow of real milk. Real milk was expensive, and there were mouths to feed. I would steady a gallon-sized plastic jug on the counter, half-filled with real milk, holding my breath, looking only at the tiny jug opening as I lifted the half-gallon pitcher of powdered milk, willing my arms not to shake so I wouldn't spill, mixing the real milk with its ghostly pretender. It always tasted gritty no matter how well it was stirred.

Soon after we moved in, Dad drove with me to the Salvation Army's second-hand store in Atlantic City—just the two of us—so I could pick out a bed and dresser. I chose a dark-wood twin headboard and a matching four-drawer dresser. It was all mine. Leslie's room was across from mine downstairs because we were the big girls. Upstairs, Liz and Lisa's room was across from my parents. That arrangement only lasted a few months. I never understood why they moved Leslie upstairs into the bedroom with Liz and Lisa, but soon it was clear that there was me and then there were "the girls." Lisa and Leslie became inseparable, and I was on my own.

Mostly, that was okay with me. I liked to keep my bedroom neat. My clothes were always folded and neatly put away. Even my crinolines were hung properly on a hanger. I made my bed every day and kept the room dusted and swept the wood floors. I needed to set a good example. When I heard my parents fighting or saw Mom sitting on the guest room bed across the hall, I closed my bedroom door and polished my dresser, willing it to shine. Mom sat facing the empty wall with a blanket over her head, reminding me of an Indian squaw from my fourth grade history book. Alone in my room, I'd straighten my cotton bedspread, and I would feel better. My sisters were not so diligent.

On 29th Street, Mom acted cranky when she had to pick up toys and clothes and books in the girls' room. The tension in the house would crackle like static electricity, and then one of us would use the wrong tone, and Mom reacted by screaming and throwing any available objects across the room. What got broken was our fault too. All kinds of things could set her off on a fury. I never knew when it might be me. She used to spank us with a wooden paddle stamped with the symbol of her college sorority. After she broke that on one of our behinds, she adopted a ping-pong paddle. The handle was sturdier, but the impact was the same.

Mom never apologized and never explained. More and more, she was becoming a mystery—a volatile and unknowable presence in the house. So, on the August Sunday in 1966 when she announced that she was going to church with us, we accepted it in silence. Preferring to sleep away the morning hours, Mom hardly ever attended church. Leslie and I were singing in the choir, while Mom sat quietly in the pews. After the service, she took us out for donuts—a nearly unheard of treat—and when we arrived home, we were turned loose to do as we pleased.

The day was hot and muggy. We were free to play at the beach or run back and forth to the house. Sometime around three o'clock, Mom walked down to the sand carrying a blanket. Usually, she would only come to the beach when accompanied by Dad or visiting relatives, everyone loaded with umbrellas, chairs, and drinks. But this day, it was just Mom in her one-piece black bathing suit. Soon she was asleep on her blanket, down near the waterline. I never thought to disturb her. It wasn't smart to wake Mom, not ever; so my sisters and I kept our distance, watching her in our peripheral vision. She stayed there, even as the tide changed and the ocean water crept up the beach toward her feet. Finally, it was Lisa who had the nerve to touch her arm. Even at six years old, Lisa was bold.

Mom still wouldn't move, so I ran home to get Dad, and he came and helped Mom off the beach. He half-carried her up the stairs to bed. A little while later, as we sat around the kitchen table, a loud *thud* told us that she had fallen out of bed. Dad called for an ambulance because she still wouldn't wake up. The ambulance, with its flashing red strobe light, alerted the neighbors and intruded into every window of our house. When the paramedics brought Mom downstairs on a stretcher, she was yelling, "Don't let them take me!" She cried and pleaded and screamed; but the men wheeled the stretcher down the front walk and into the ambulance, shut the door firmly, and pulled away into the night. The crazy red light receded, and quiet took its place. A neighbor came over to stay with us until the morning.

This thus began our longest separation. Mom was in and out of hospitals for the next year as doctors and therapists tried to fix the damage she had inflicted upon her internal organs. She had taken a lot of pills—mostly Seconal, a powerful barbiturate—although apparently she didn't lack variety. Some parts of her digestive system shut down, and the doctors had to remove one of her kidneys. She was committed to the psychiatric hospital at Temple University, but she still wasn't getting better. Later, the doctors realized she had a raging infection because the surgeon left a sponge inside Mom when he removed her kidney. She had to have a colostomy bag for a full year after that surgery. She was only thirty-two years old. I was nine. As the oldest, I took over a lot of the cooking chores, helped Dad with bills and scheduling, bossed my sisters around, and tried to keep the house clean while desperately attempting to keep order.

Luckily, I had Brigantine. We all did. And for the weeks when Mom was too sick to be with us and Dad needed to be with her, we were farmed out to neighbors and friends. If you stood in front of our house on 29th Street, you could practically hit the different houses we stayed in with a stone. The island of Brigantine was just four miles long and four or five blocks wide, so nothing was too far away. If you stood on a standard A-frame ladder in the middle of Brigantine Avenue, you could see the Atlantic Ocean over one shoulder and the inlet bay over the other.

In 1940, there were 403 people living on the island full time. By 1970, the population swelled to about seven thousand, and it still seemed that everyone knew everyone else's business. So whenever paramedics came or another incident sent Mom to the hospital, neighboring families set another place for dinner.

Leslie, younger than me by twelve months and two weeks, usually stayed with Reverend McNaughton and his family. Fair-haired and sunny, Leslie was the girl who sang sweetly to herself and caught on to everything so quickly that she taught me some of life's basic skills. I clearly remember Leslie teaching me to read the face of a clock or sitting on the steps offering to teach me how to tie my shoes. "This bunny ear wraps around that bunny ear." She laughed easily and often.

In sixth grade, Leslie was awarded a medal for the best all-around Girl Scout, and I still remember the jealous sting of not getting it myself. Leslie was so bright and good-natured; sending her to the McNaughtons might have been one last attempt by my dad to build a better reputation for us in Brigantine. The Reverend James McNaughton, I remember, was a burly man with a petite wife named Mary. The church provided them a split-level house on 28th Street; and they filled it with two adopted daughters and a huge, shaggy, drooling Newfoundland that routinely knocked over the furniture just by wagging its tail. Island churchgoers attended either the Community Presbyterian Church, mid-island at 15th Street, or St. Thomas Catholic Church further south on 8th Street.

Then there was Lisa. Square jawed and dark eyed, she was twenty-two months younger than Leslie. Often during Mom's absences, Lisa stayed with her first-grade teacher, Mrs. Billie Raye, with whom she had an affinity. There was something special about Billie Raye because Lisa had chased off so many babysitters. Lisa was Mom's favorite, but she wasn't an easy kid. She had the kind of determined willfulness that made for loud and long tantrums. If flailing her limbs didn't work, she would hold her breath until she turned blue. I have a clear early memory of Lisa—maybe three or four years old—lying on her back furiously pounding her feet and hands into the living room carpet and then, in front of an astonished babysitter, clamping her mouth closed and slowly turning blue around her lips and under her eyes. Then she passed out. Once that furious will of hers was unconscious, she breathed. We never saw that babysitter again. Cousin Betty Lou, who babysat often when we lived in Fords, claimed that Lisa was the only child who frightened her because of her breath-holding tactics.

Mom had a favorite story about Lisa. In kindergarten, a teacher asked Lisa to please pick up some toys. Lisa shot back, "If you want them picked up, you pick them up." She was five years old. Mom loved Lisa's gall. That girl wouldn't take guff off anyone, Mom said. When Lisa was tested by the school district and her IQ came back as 155, Mom crowed. After that Lisa was special, almost magical as if she possessed some extra fragility or power due to her massive intellect. So, if Lisa threw a tantrum about doing the dishes, Mom let her off the hook. If Lisa didn't want to set the table, that was okay too. Either Leslie or I would be assigned to do it. When Lisa behaved badly in school, it was the school's fault. Poor Lisa was bored.

Billie Raye, though, seemed to understand Lisa. Billie Raye was a big woman with a pretty face, an overgrown garden, and a much smaller husband. Their two college-aged daughters lived away, so I thought Lisa would have been bored there, but Lisa did not rebel about being shuffled off to another house until we all did.

It's telling that I can't really remember where Liz stayed during the weeks that we were farmed out. Two years behind Lisa in school, Liz was the youngest and very quiet. She had a talent for ducking under the chaos and withdrawing into her room at just the right time. Most likely, Liz stayed with Maurice and Linda Cole, who lived across the street and just a few houses down.

Maurie Cole was a corporate lawyer, an avid golfer, and a hard drinker. He always had a pitcher of martinis in the freezer, ready any time of the day. I loved his wife, Linda, who kept an orderly home. She sprayed Maurie's pillowcase with lavender water before ironing it. She said it helped Maurie sleep better. I remember long afternoons following her around the house or being her mother's helper—putting away dishes, wiping off the table, or sweeping the floor. Linda always remembered my birthday in March and took me shopping for some special item—a hand-painted lamp or a quilted bedspread. I don't think she was close with Liz like that, but as a mother of three adopted children, she was always willing to take in another child.

I stayed with the Rogges—a fact that changed all our lives. I was best friends with Lee Rogge from the first year we lived in Brigantine. Lee and I had the same name and the same hair color and both loved animals and climbing trees, and she was good in math—the only subject I found really difficult. Lee's parents, John and Betsy, had practically built the town up in the years following World War II.

I knew their story by heart. John and Betsy met in college in New York City and were dating when John was called to Navy duty. Betsy stayed behind, employed as a nurse in Bellevue. In 1944, John's ship pulled into Miami for a forty-eight-hour shore leave. He had written Betsy ahead of time, asking her to meet him in Florida and marry him. When his ship pulled into port, his heart was in his mouth, not knowing if Betsy got his letter, whether she would be there, and if she would marry him. When they spotted each other on the crowded dock, both knew they would be together forever.

Two years later, they moved to Brigantine where Betsy's father had a real estate development company. The town went bankrupt that same year and was taken over by the state, which in turn sold five thousand empty house lots to Betsy's dad. John joined the real estate company and became Brigantine's biggest booster. It took twenty years to sell those lots and populate the town of Brigantine. By then, John had been elected mayor.

Betsy and John raised four children of their own in those early years and then added two daughters of a close friend when the girls needed a home. By the time I was staying with the Rogges, Lee and one older sister were the only ones home; and it was a peaceful kingdom, that house on 27th Street. With lots of windows, clean, white clapboard siding, and black shutters—real ones, not decorative—the house had well-trimmed gardens all around and a koi pond under a weeping willow. Inside the house, Oriental rugs decorated gleaming hardwood floors, art covered the walls, and books and glossy magazines rested on the antique furniture. In the summer, the Oriental rugs were carefully put away, and jute or sisal rugs appeared in their places. Betsy Rogge worked as a nurse and did a lot of volunteering, so she usually wasn't home until late in the afternoon. I remember tables littered with the paperwork of causes, charity balls, and a campaign for reducing worldwide population growth, shuffled together with flyers announcing the women's club annual mixer.

In the morning, Betsy always took something out of the freezer for dinner. There would be a roast or pork chops or chicken sitting on the counter or in the refrigerator, thawing. On mornings, she had deliveries from the milkman, the egg man, the bread man, and the fruit and vegetable man. They even had a donut man. All of them would walk in the back door, check the refrigerator or pantry to see what was needed, and restock. You never knew who might be in the kitchen. In the late afternoon, Betsy would curl up on the couch with a book—often a Harlequin Romance novel—and often wouldn't leap up to make dinner until she heard John's tires crunching in the driveway promptly at 5:00 p.m.

A person could set a watch by John Rogge. He was a real estate agent with his office in a prominent building near the main traffic circle in town. Breakfast was ready at 7:00 a.m., and dinner was served at 6:00 p.m. unless he had a meeting. By 1958, John was a member of the three-person city council and twelve years later was elected mayor, so he attended just about every civic function in Brigantine and knew everyone by name. No matter how many pancake breakfasts or Kiwanis Club Awards dinners he had to attend, though, he was always home in the evening by 5:00 p.m. to have one glass of wine before dinner or to pick up Betsy if they were going out. He played tennis several mornings a week and was always home in bed by 11:00 p.m.

When Lee and I got hungry, we ate Klondike ice-cream bars with impunity. There were cookies and milk and usually a leftover homemade cake or pie from Sunday dinner.

We never studied at my house. On 29th Street, I never knew what Mom would be up to, so I didn't invite anyone over. Sometimes, there was a seasonal wreath hanging on the front door and a roast cooking in the oven, and Mom would laugh and talk about her plans for an upcoming holiday or party. She would tell me about the dresses she was going to make for us and ask about my grades at school. Mostly, though, the house was filled with a dead quiet; and I would tiptoe through the rooms, both looking for and trying to avoid my mother. On a good quiet day, she would be passed out on the bed. On a bad quiet day, she would be passed out on the floor in the utility room, beneath a four-inch hole in the wall and a smear of blood. On these quiet days, I learned to start looking for something to fix for dinner. There was never something delicious defrosting on our counter.

The Rogges lived by schedules. They made promises and kept them. When I stayed with them, I started a habit of doing extra chores—mopping the kitchen or dusting the living room—without being asked. I think the Rogges appreciated it. I always kept my room neat and scrubbed clean, so it felt natural when I picked up a broom or dustrag like I did at home. I just wanted to be helpful, which wasn't really necessary because their maid Eleanor cleaned weekly. All I wanted was to stay there and be part of a normal family.

I still think about those few square blocks of Brigantine in the 1960s. The sidewalks and beaches, the houses, and the families who lived there were my whole world in a way that my daughter will never understand. We didn't just move into the neighborhood. Those blocks shaped and defined our expectations about life, burrowed into our dreams, and gave us a sense of self. We were welcomed into Brigantine because we were four little girls with nice manners. I think people felt sorry for us, and when the neighbors helped us, they felt good about themselves.

My mother had a harder time fitting in. Not long ago, on a visit back to Brigantine, Linda Cole told me a story I keep coming back to. Linda is still nearly as pretty and blonde, as perfectly matched and certain as she was back then, and is too kind to say anything overtly derogatory. But she did tell me the story about her meeting my mother for the first time. The Coles were having a costume party that was already in full swing when she heard a knock at the door. Since all her guests were present, she opened the door reluctantly to find my mother, alone, on her front step.

"Well, hi," Mom said. "I'm your new neighbor. We just moved in, and since you're having a party, I thought I'd come over and introduce myself."

Of course, Linda invited her in, but it was scandalous all the same. Linda made that point clear in the set of her eyebrows as she told the story. Linda and Maurie had money and a membership in the Brigantine Country Club. They were friends with all the "best" people on the island. I imagine Mom was a bit tipsy and without Dad was hoping to come off as fun and daring, but she just seemed desperate. It was a foreign emotion; but I actually felt sorry for Mom, imagining her standing on that doorstep, within view of her own house but an utter stranger, trying to fit in.

1974

AFTER THE FIRE

We all live in a house on fire, no fire department
to call, no way out, just the upstairs window
to look out while the fire burns the house
down with us trapped, locked in it.
                                        —Tennessee Williams

Tragedy. Like a magnet, it attracts. Like iron chips drawn — no, compelled — to respond to a magnet's pull, tragedy pulls people to it. Any day. Any hour. An irresistible lure. The curious, thrill seekers and the bored. They all come. There is no apathy at scenes of tragedy and grief. Watch the crowds. See their eyes transfixed on scenes better left unseen. Drownings. Accidents. Fires. Fires. One of the most tragic ways of death. Crowds, fascinated, push against police lines to get a better look. At the scene. And at the bodies. The bodies. Even the sanctity of death, the final silent dignity, does not immediately come. It must wait for the last curiosity to be satisfied. Until the ambulance finally leaves. As it did in Ventnor Friday.

News photo, Atlantic City Press, *June 22, 1974*

My sisters and I were interviewed separately twice in June and July
of 1974, the fire investigation reports showed, and our stories were
mostly consistent. I didn't remember who interviewed us first, within
a day or two of the fire. The two-page report was unsigned. But that

investigator set the tone for anyone else reading the file when he wrote: "*Strictly Confidential*—Mother was heavy drinker and used tranquilizers frequently—stayed up late at night and slept during the day."

Even today, I felt the sting of shame. I wanted to protest that she had been taking her Antabuse medication and it had been more than a month since her last suicide attempt. She was trying to get better. But my words were weak against that capitalized stage whisper: *Don't tell anybody, but Mom is a drunk.*

At least my sisters and I sounded reasonably competent in the reports. Lisa and I woke about the same time that night, we said in separate statements, and noticed the thick gray smoke. We never saw each other inside the house, but the first thing we both remembered hearing was my mother on the telephone, calling the police. "Help me!" she yelled. "The whole house is on fire." Lisa woke Leslie and practically pulled her, dopey with sleep, to the window in the middle bedroom where Lisa jumped onto the grassy lawn, followed by Leslie. I ran into that smoke-filled hallway too, with Liz trailing, trying to get to our parents; but the heat pushed Liz and I back into our bedroom.

I jumped out the window. Then the three of us gathered below urging Liz to jump. She cried, "I can't. I'm only twelve years old." I said I would catch her, but I didn't. When she finally pushed away from the windowsill, arms and legs flailing, we saw the orange flames pulsating behind her in the bedroom window. We yelled for our parents, but we never did see or hear them alive again.

I had a faded newspaper clipping from the *Atlantic City Press*, June 22, 1974. The headline said, "Parents Die, Save Kids in Blaze." I wanted that to be true. Everyone wanted my parents to be heroes, especially since they were dead. Of the four of us, only Liz claimed to have heard my parents shouting to us that night, urging us to get out of the house. She heard Mom and Dad both, she told the investigator, yelling at her to jump off that window ledge. But I was sure they were already dead by then. Mom was found on the floor at the foot of the bed. Dad was lying next to the bathtub that he was trying to fill with water.

Dad was a volunteer firefighter, back in Fords, and had drilled us all in escape routes and lifesaving measures. I guess he thought he could ride out the fire in a bathtub of water. It's funny, though, that he didn't do the first and most obvious thing: closing the doors. The doors to their bedroom and bathroom were both wide open. When the flames reached the top of the stairs, a fire report said, the flames surged into my parents' wide-open room and rushed across the floor to the open window to join the rest of the fire outside. The fire acted like a freight train passing, sucking all the oxygen behind it so there was nothing left for Dad or Mom to breathe.

Outside the house that night, it was bedlam. Firemen from Ventnor Heights arrived first, followed by Ventnor City and Atlantic City responding to a general alarm with one pumper, one aerial truck, and firefighting apparatus. The trucks couldn't fit in the U-shaped parking lot where the only fire hydrant was blocked by illegally parked cars. Spectators lined up, jarred from their beds at 3:00 a.m. by the ear-piercing sirens.

In the reports, Leslie and Lisa described watching me run up onto the flaming front porch, trying to get back to our parents. I did not make it past the threshold. The ambulance arrived, its beaconing flashing lights reminding me once again of the troubles we had in Brigantine. Liz's arm was badly burned, so the paramedics transported all of us girls to the hospital together. I barely remembered what happened after being forced back from the porch. I was numb, probably in shock. People spoke to me. I responded, but nothing sank in. I did what I was told. The nurses could have announced that my mother had risen from the dead, and I would have accepted that as just one more thing.

Lisa, on the other hand, was angry. The nurses were dumb; their questions were stupid. When they asked for her name and address, Lisa told them she didn't have an address anymore. Weren't they paying attention? They asked Lisa for her parents' names. She shot back, "What for? They're dead. It's like crying over spilled milk."

The reports noted that John Rogge, mayor of Brigantine, took us home from the hospital just before dawn, back through Atlantic City and over the bridge into Brigantine, which we never should have left. John and Betsy had become accustomed to saving us girls—and especially me—over the years. They set us up with blankets and pillows on the sofas in the living room. The first night of summer came to a shattered end, taking our family with it, muting our childhood innocence, changing our lives forever.

Since we escaped from the fire with nothing but our nightgowns, Betsy put out the word asking for clothing donations. The good people of Brigantine and around the county responded with carloads of stuff—clothes, bedding, books, and more clothes in all kinds of crazy sizes. Betsy spent a lot of time in the garage, sweating in her blouses and shorts as she sorted. Then, she ushered us girls downstairs to select new clothes from the piles of clothes that were deemed appropriate. Still, more donations came—dropped off on the Rogges driveway in piles and bags until Betsy complained that she would never be able to dig out.

Upstairs in the air-conditioned living room, Betsy organized us to catalogue all our possessions that had been lost in the fire, for insurance purposes. We worked together to write a letter to be read at our parents' funeral. We also had to make decisions about what to do with their bodies, answering questions as best we could. Mom wanted to be cremated, we said. Dad wanted to be buried in his family's cemetery plot in Perth Amboy. Our parents never seemed to agree on anything, and there we were, again, stuck between them.

Betsy shook her short, practical hair and asked, "Well, how about if we put your mom's ashes into a pretty box and bury it in the casket with your dad?"

She reached under the ledge of the fireplace hearth and brought out a lovely carved, wooden box. It was ideal. Who had the perfect box for cremated remains just lying around like that? In that moment, I wanted to be like Aunt Betsy.

Aunt Betsy kept us informed about developments in the case, telling us that a special arson investigator was looking into our fire, a detective named Walter Buzby. Betsy told us that the fire left burn patterns that seemed to indicate an accelerant had been used. We needed to think about who might have done this, Betsy said. We should be prepared to take polygraph tests. I could still remember politely thanking Betsy for keeping us informed. Lisa just ran off again.

On July 3, a police detective, Sergeant Gilbert, and Deputy Fire Marshal William Rutley interviewed the four of us again. Even after all these years, I could see my annoyance spilling over on the pages of these transcripts, which was a little surprising because I was always a good girl and respectful around authority. They wanted to know what time I got home, whether my sisters were home, and if we had boys in the house. Who smoked in the house? Was the air conditioning on? Had there been any other fires—small fires that perhaps we did not report? Or fires at our last house in Brigantine?

> Sgt. Gilbert: To the best of your knowledge, was anyone smoking, either in the den or the living room or any part of the house, when you went to bed?
>
> Leigh: When I came in, my parents were sitting on the couch together.
>
> Sgt. Gilbert: Where at, in the den or the…
>
> Leigh: In the den and I came in and looked at the hope chest that my father had just taken off the varnish. He had sanded it and not to my knowledge was she (my mother) smoking.
>
> Sgt. Gilbert: How about the doors, where they locked when you came in to go to bed?
>
> Leigh: No, open.
>
> Sgt. Gilbert: And you left them open?
>
> Leigh: Yes, I just walked in.
>
> Sgt. Gilbert. Let me ask you another question. Did you ever have any other fires while you were at Burk Court, fires that you didn't report? Like, small fires?
>
> Leigh: In the house? No.
>
> Sgt. Gilbert: How about in Brigantine, where you lived before?
>
> Leigh: No.

> Sgt. Gilbert: No fires over there either?
>
> Leigh: No, no.

My answers were increasingly short. I did not know what time my sisters got home that night. There were no boys in the house. We did not have money to run the air conditioning. No fires. No.

Then they went back to the chemicals. Dad did not have a job that summer, so he was refinishing furniture around the house. I knew what the investigators thought—flammable chemicals lying around, a hot night, an open door, or boys running around outside. Dad never left chemicals lying around. He was fastidious about putting all his tools and supplies away in the utility closet.

I told the investigators this, but they just kept hammering about those chemicals. Then they focused on whether our RCA color television had an "instant on" feature or if the set had to warm up before you got a picture, which was ridiculous because even I knew the television did not set the fire; a person did. Aunt Betsy and the respected fire investigator, Walter Buzby, said so. Shouldn't they ask me about Lisa? But they never did.

I laid down the reports for a minute and saw it again: a person splashing a murderous liquid over the threshold of my parent's bedroom door, moving on to mine, sloshing it down the hall, but stopping just short of Lisa and Leslie's bedroom door. The investigators were asking the wrong questions. And they kept asking the wrong questions. Here was Leslie:

> Leslie: We were screaming to my sister, Liz to jump out the window and she finally jumped and we were all screaming to my parents. I think it was around 3:15, something like that. I'm pretty sure that it was.
>
> Sgt. Gilbert: What makes you so sure it was around that time?
>
> Leslie: Because Lisa and I ran around back, ran around the back of the house, it was around

> 3:20, I believe it was. She told me it was
> around 3:20.
>
> Sgt. Gilbert: Did she have a watch on?
>
> Leslie: Yes, she had a watch on.

Lisa had a watch on? Did she sleep with it on or put it on her wrist after she woke up, before jumping out the window? I didn't remember any of us sleeping with watches on. I picked up Lisa's interview:

> Deputy Rutley: You had talked to your sister…
> about the possibility of sneaking out (that
> night).
>
> Lisa: Yeah, to tell you the truth, I wasn't going
> to tell you this, but do you think I started
> the fire?
>
> Deputy Rutley: No, I just want to hear every-
> thing, I want you to tell us everything.

Encouraged, Lisa went on to tell the detectives all about going out drinking on the Boardwalk on the evening of June 20. She had some pot because her boyfriend had given her a dime bag for her eighth grade graduation and she finished it up on the beach that night with another boy she just met. When she got home, she tried to talk Leslie into sneaking out with her after curfew, but Leslie fell asleep. Lisa usually jumped out a window around 1:00 a.m., she told Rutley, to meet some boys living in the Waterview townhouses and get high.

Within the next two weeks, according to the reports, the mother of one of Leslie's friends called Fire Marshall Rutley to report that Leslie was heard saying, "They're dead. We're free now."

Then the principal at Lisa's middle school called Detective Joseph Fields to report a story he heard. The kids were saying that Lisa asked Joey C. about how to start a fire, Principal Kelly said. Also, Lisa was getting some kind of psychiatric help at the guidance center. Maybe Detective Fields could check that out, Principal Kelly said.

My sisters and I all remembered Detective Fields. We used to call him Joe Friday because he always wore a suit and tried to act cool, even though his clothes and his hair and everything about him was square. Fields worked narcotics, so all the kids knew him. They said he had a snitch at the high school and maybe at the middle school too. He liked to show up at kids' houses, whether their parents were home or not, and demand to look around their bedrooms. He came to our house at least once that I remembered, before the fire. I called my dad to the door, and he looked at Detective Fields standing there and said something like, "You again." Lisa was always in trouble by then. It was humiliating.

After Mom and Dad died, I thought Lisa might settle down, but losing everything and moving to the Rogges just seemed to make her more defiant. One day that summer, just a couple of weeks after the fire, Aunt Betsy came home in the afternoon to find strange cars in the driveway and her mother, Mutti, waiting for her near the front door.

Mutti lived in her own apartment downstairs in John and Betsy's fourplex. She was an impressive woman, her clothes sewn from rich fabrics, perfectly tailored, and her fingers always glittered with diamonds and gold, topped with manicured shell-pink fingernails. Her collection of furs she wore reminded us of Eva Gabor on the red carpet.

On this day, Mutti had tears in her eyes.

"The girls have some friends visiting," Mutti said. "Those sweet children are all upstairs, grieving with those girls and as quiet as can be."

Aunt Betsy opened the door and was greeted by a cloud of marijuana smoke. Horrified because she knew Uncle John, the mayor of Brigantine, was due to be home soon, she ordered the kids to go home and called the parents she knew. Leslie and Lisa were in trouble, but they were not terribly impressed by that. Leslie was politely chastened, at least. But Lisa showed no emotion.

Those few summer weeks while we were all together were a memory wrapped in thick fuzzy wool. Liz's arm was bandaged from her burns. My throat was still sore. Leslie and Lisa whispered a lot. They were fourteen and sixteen and gone whenever they could be, running off to get high and hang out on the Boardwalk with their friends in Atlantic City and Ventnor.

By late July, Lisa wouldn't listen to anyone. After dinner one night, Aunt Betsy told Lisa it was her turn to load the dishes into the washer. Lisa said, "No." Betsy said this wasn't a negotiation; it was Lisa's turn. Lisa snapped "Fuck off" and then ran down the stairs and out the front door.

Uncle John ran after Lisa, down the stairs and out onto the driveway just in time to see fourteen-year-old Lisa stick her thumb out to the cars on Atlantic Brigantine Boulevard, heading into Atlantic City. A car with a man driving stopped. Lisa hopped in, and she was gone.

Betsy spent half the night on the telephone, trying to find Lisa. She was sleeping under someone's pool table when they found her. The Rogges called our Aunt Jill and Uncle Doug in Fords. They packed Lisa's things and drove her north on Garden State Parkway to a Howard Johnson's restaurant, where they met Jill and Doug who were waiting to take her to their home. When the Rogges returned without Lisa, the house was quiet, finally. I was just glad Lisa was gone.

The Rogges arranged for me to receive counseling that summer from a respected New York psychiatrist who bought their former house on 27th Street from Uncle John. In their old sunroom, where I used to read magazines just to be near Aunt Betsy while she worked through a pile of correspondence at her desk, the kindly, bespectacled Dr. Counts taught me about Elisabeth Kübler-Ross and the five stages of grief from her book *On Death and Dying*. I studied hard and memorized each stage, determined to be prepared for the next emotion that would come.

Aunt Betsy generously invited me to stay at their house in order to finish my senior year in high school. She persuaded me to find a project to occupy myself for the rest of that summer. Every morning, she said we needed to wake up, get dressed, and make a plan for the day. I just needed a goal, Betsy said; and since I was pretty, I should enter the Miss Brigantine contest that was only six weeks away.

Of course I was flattered. In the eighth grade, I enrolled in McCullough's Modeling School for six consecutive Saturdays, paid for with my own babysitting money, so I already knew how to pivot on a runway. I learned from Mrs. Bill Faunce, our high school principal's wife and a former model, the ten-point system for dressing—how every item one wore, whether clothing or jewelry, counted for a point. Jackie O was nearly always a perfect 7. I knew to cross my ankles, not my legs, when I sat. While I was clearly too short to model, I knew I could still work at that unassailable veneer that beautiful women had, the perfect sheen of invulnerability.

I resumed my jobs cleaning houses and babysitting. I made my daily plans. And for two weeks that summer, I had rehearsals and a shopping trip for an evening gown to wear in the Miss Brigantine contest. I shoved my grief deep inside me.

Atlantic City was the Mecca for beauty contests back then. The competitions to become Miss Atlantic City and Miss Atlantic County—both very prestigious—were covered in the *Atlantic City Press* for several days running. Front-page stories previewing the talent offerings of a group of eighteen-year-old girls were common. The Miss Brigantine contest made the paper twice. In a preview-of-the-contest story, a murky photograph showed a half-dozen of us grouped around a piano as if we were all about to burst into song. The story mentioned nothing of the fire.

Nobody said anything about the fire. I was a pretty girl, not a tragic one. Since I could not sing, play piano, or twirl a baton, I worried that I did not have a talent. Betsy reminded me that I could sew and write, so I did. I sewed a simple A-line shift dress in a cream silk and wrote a poem about loss. Our chaperones took us shopping for gowns at an Atlantic City boutique. We practiced walking on the runway—the pivot and smile. I didn't remember the pageant itself, but the headline in the *Press* read, "250 People Shocked by Tie," because the judges could not decide between all the pretty girls and declared there were two winners. One of the winners was Sally Plum, whose family owned the funeral home where my parents had been laid out six weeks earlier.

As second runner up, I supposed I came in fourth. I was just thrilled to have my name announced. Maybe that sounded like the polite lie of a loser. It wasn't.

During the days after Jessica and I visited the Waterview town-homes, when I decided to reopen this investigation, we stayed with the Rogges in Brigantine. Pacing the carpeted halls one morning, feeling like I couldn't catch a full breath, I noticed that my old trophies were no longer in their niche near the stairs. Aunt Betsy directed me to the garage—which I still remembered as being stuffed with the charity of our neighbors—and I discovered them on a dusty back shelf, with flaking gold paint: *2nd Runner-Up Miss Brigantine, 1974*; *Miss Caesars Boardwalk Regency, 1979*; and *Miss Atlantic City, 1980*. This was my old armor against feeling like a nobody, a victim of circumstances, chaff in the wind. I dusted the trophies off and shipped them back to California, because one never knew when she would need that armor again.

I tried to remember the day of the Miss Brigantine pageant as exciting and fun, but really, I didn't remember much at all. I was numb that whole summer, and without emotions to help stick memories against my internal walls, the recollections slipped away. I kept moving, going from housecleaning jobs to babysitting. I spent time with my steady boyfriend, Allan, and his family in Atlantic City. I crossed my ankles when I sat. I kept my room clean. I minded my manners.

Now, I started thinking about where I could locate the documents that survived the fire. There were some old letters between Mom and her family, I remembered, and some paperwork about her hospitalization. I wondered if any of the original investigators were still alive. I started to write things down. Throughout my life, I had used writing to organize my thoughts, to name my emotions and control them. Now I started writing to raise my memories, to hold them up to the light, shake off the dust, and truly examine my past.

I was scared of my compulsion to unearth the past and the mess I might be creating. Messes worried me. I could not turn away, even if I had to follow the ghost of my drunken mother through those dark hallways, even if I had to follow Lisa into the chaos that always seemed to surround her. I was determined to know what happened.

2009

INVESTIGATION

Monsters are real and ghosts are real too. They
live inside us, and sometimes they win.

—Stephen King

On the flight back to Atlantic City, I resisted the lure of the novel in
my bag and turned again to the pages of supplementary investigation
reports, mostly written by Detective Fields. It's funny that Fields, our
Joe Friday teen narcotics detective, was assigned to investigate our
fire. Maybe he worked the case because he knew the kids involved.
Maybe the Ventnor Police Department (PD) just didn't have anyone
trained in arson investigations. It was a small-town police station.

Now, finally, after long months pouring over these police and
fire reports, praying the truth would leap off the pages, I was going to
meet the man who wrote them. It was Lisa who actually located him.
A few months earlier, I made copies of these reports for my sisters as
Christmas gifts, but only Lisa took a real interest. She was clever with
Internet searches; and she learned Detective Joseph Fields, past pres-
ident of the New Jersey Narcotic Enforcement Officers Association,
was being honored at Trump Plaza in Atlantic City. I booked a flight.

Lisa said she was anxious to clear her name. Being uncertain of
her real motives, I did not tell her I was flying east and that Detective
Fields had agreed to meet with me. I did not tell John and Betsy I
would be there either. I just couldn't. I was convinced Fields knew
who killed my parents; he just couldn't put it in writing because he
was told to stop investigating. I felt close enough to touch the truth

and feel its rough texture in my hand. It was all there in the file. I began reading the first supplementary report.

A joint investigation of the Ventnor City fire and police departments was formally launched on July 1, 1974. Detective Joseph Fields and Fire Marshall William Rutley began by going door-to-door in the Waterview townhomes. Eleven days had passed since the fire, so speculation and rumor had already metastasized. What the maintenance man heard from Mrs. Goldstein became the memory of Mrs. Kearney's daughter. People definitely heard two of those Overton girls that night joking around outside the fire, talking about something trivial like leaving two dollars in a cabinet. They laughed while their parents burned.

All that day, eleven days after the fire, from 3:00 p.m. until almost 10:00 p.m., Fields and Rutley knocked on doors, asking questions. Around 7:30 p.m., they talked with Bill W. on Marshall court. Bill was fifteen years old and admitted being one of the boys whom everybody heard that night. Keith D. and George D., both thirteen years old, told the same story. They had been hanging around the parking lot for a while and then walked over to the J. M. Fields department store. They returned to Waterview about 1:00 a.m., watched television at Bill's house, and were in bed asleep by 2:30 a.m. Keith reported that on the way home from J. M. Fields, he happened to glance up and see Lisa's bedroom light on. She was walking around up there, but that was all he saw.

A Mr. Silvagni said he came home at 2:55 a.m., just twenty minutes before Mom called the fire department. Mr. Silvagni stated that the town houses were quiet. He parked on the street and walked into the complex. It was a nice night, he said. He went inside his apartment, just across the way from ours, had a cigarette, watched a little television, and had just started brushing his teeth before bed when he heard a loud bang. That must have been our windows exploding, I guess.

Mrs. Goldstein heard that bang too. She looked out her second-floor window and saw three boys running away from the fire, yelling "Oh, mama! Oh, mama!" as they sped off, heading toward the bay, she reported.

And then there was this: On July 11, 1974, Atlantic County Fire Investigator Walter Buzby called the Ventnor City Police Department and talked to the lieutenant detective, according to a note in the file. Buzby requested the lieutenant to halt all investigation into the Overton case because Buzby and Detective Fields were going to "interview some people tomorrow and…blow this case wide open and bring it to a successful conclusion."

Two days later, on July 13, 1974, Fields and Buzby brought in Lisa and her friend Beth for another interview. The girls were interviewed separately. John and Betsy Rogge were present for Lisa's interrogation, if that's the right word. It read more like a friendly chat.

Lisa told the same story about the night of the fire—where she was on the Boardwalk with Beth and got home about a half hour before her midnight curfew. She was high on marijuana and called up to Leslie through an open bedroom window, trying to get Les to come outside to use up her last half hour of freedom. But Dad heard the girls through the den's open window and made Lisa come inside. She went to bed. When she woke up, the house was on fire.

Fields asked Lisa a lot of questions about pot in that interview—how much she smoked, where she got it, how high she was. He was, after all, a narcotics detective. Lisa said she never took pills and didn't even like aspirin. She smoked something called African *keiba* the night of the fire and was feeling mellow, she said. Lisa told the same story of escaping the fire, but they didn't dwell on it. They talked again about the chemicals Dad used to refinish furniture. Lisa said he was always careful about putting chemicals back in the utility room and the fire, she reminded Buzby and Fields, didn't start there. They never asked Lisa if she wanted her parents dead. They didn't ask her if she started the fire.

Beth's story was the same as Lisa's, except she said there was always fighting going on at the Overton house between Mom and Dad and us girls. According to her, my mom was a nag. She said I always sided with Mom against Lisa. My sisters hated me, Beth said. I read this section over again and felt the sting of those words every time.

Beth admitted they didn't take a bus home from the Boardwalk that night. They hitchhiked. Fields scolded Beth about that. He told her if it was late at night and no rides were available, she should call the police department. Beth said, "Cops don't help you." That same day of the interview, seven hours later, Beth showed up alone at the police station around 9:30 p.m. and said she missed the last bus and needed to get to Brigantine. Detective Fields reported giving her a ride.

Somewhere in among the reports, barely noticed, my plane landed. I collected my small bag and found a cab for the ride into town. It reeked of cigarettes and mildew. Twenty minutes later, I was temporarily blinded by the midday white sidewalk in front of Trump Plaza. It was a bright day in Atlantic City, where light bounced off the ocean and up the alleys. I remembered wishing for a pair of sunglasses during the summer of 1974 down on the Boardwalk, and that was before all the glass towers were erected that reflected even more light.

Standing on the sidewalk, I let my eyes adjust and looked for landmarks like the ratty old arcade at Texas Avenue and the Boardwalk where my sisters hung out, smoking pot and playing pinball. But that too was gone.

I had a job on the Boardwalk that summer of 1974, doing light clerical work in an auction house near the Texas Avenue arcade. The owners called it an auction house, but it was what we used to call a jam joint. Its sole business was to lure sun-addled tourists with the promise of cheap, high-quality souvenirs and small appliances. The owners, Kathy and Abe, lived near us in the Waterview townhomes. I cleaned their house, and Kathy liked me, so she offered me a summer job in the back room of their Boardwalk business.

Their auction house was wedged into a small storefront, between a saltwater taffy shop and sundries store that sold post cards and sweat shirts printed with "I Love Atlantic City." A few blocks further north, tourists would shake the hand of a life-size statue of Mr. Peanut which greeted them outside Peanut World, where a bag of warm roasted peanuts was exchanged for their hard-earned money.

Across the way, another stand sold fresh-squeezed lemonade, pink cotton candy, and Nathan's hot dogs.

Right in front of the auction house, Abe would position a good-looking college guy or two, talking fast to the tourists and showing off our great watches and television sets. They suckered people by promising top quality; but what they got later in the mail was cheap, broken, or fake. Later, the tourist would figure out they got ripped off and write letters of complaint. My job was to sort the bills from the complaints and then offer exchanges and apologies to the unhappy customers, knowing the mark would never send the cheap stuff back and we never refunded a dime.

I hated that place. The back office was small and dingy. The whole building reeked of dust and despair. I used the excuse of my parents' death to never go back. Places like that were dinosaurs now. Back then, people who got suckered were embarrassed—they just lost a game everybody knew we were playing. People tended to accept their fates and their mistakes. Today, there would be outrage, headlines, and lawsuits.

Inside Trump Plaza was mercifully cool. The atmosphere was flashy and bright, a place where reward bells clanged and time stopped. Pulling money out of people's pockets was cleaner and more efficient now. Just before I was crowned Miss Atlantic City 1980, I gave a speech about how great casinos would be for the economic vitality of the community. The truth was I didn't like them much. Casinos made me anxious and sad, as if those bells rang each time a retiree lost their pension to the slot machines and flashing lights. Still, I followed the white placards to the annual meeting of the Narcotic Enforcement Officers Association. My eyes jumped from face to face, one hand firm on my leather carry bag filled with notes and questions.

I prepared for this meeting the same way I studied for college exams. I read and reread these pages countless times, memorizing as much as I could jimmy into my brain. Dad's CO_2 saturation was 46.4 percent, while Mom's was 80.8 percent. Lisa and Leslie had talked about sneaking out that night. Lisa wore a watch to bed. Several people reported hearing a boom, boys laughing, and tires squealing. Where were the color photographs of the pour patterns charred into the floor? My notes and questions were neatly laid out in notebooks and photocopies. Every step I took across that gold and black swirled carpet was bringing me closer to the truth.

Detective Fields shuffled across that carpet very slowly. A man at his elbow helped him take the few steps from the doorway of the empty conference room to a banquet table where I was sitting. Fields appeared much larger than I remembered. The other man, who introduced himself only as "a friend of Joe," told me not to tire the detective because he would be accepting a big award that night. He stepped back toward the door and waited.

Fields didn't meet my eyes as I smiled and nodded and hoped that I looked sympathetic. "I just got outta the hospital," Detective Fields began, the words thick in his mouth. "I had a heart attack, and now I'm tired."

Fields was the kind of fat that always looked rumpled and exhausted. His hair was still thick and a quiet shade of white, but his face was pallid gray. I was so grateful to be in his presence I encouraged him to talk about his medical issues. It turned out that's all he wanted to talk about—the hospital and his symptoms and what the doctor said that week.

"A fire? No. I don't remember any fire," he said, looking down at the thick veins roping over the tops of his hands, spotted with liver-colored blotches. "What was the name again?"

"Overton. Maybe you remember my sister? Lisa Overton?" A fluttering of panic began in the base of my throat. "She was… You came to our house a few times."

"Oh sure, sure," Fields said, finally meeting my eye. "She was around those boys, Stuart and Joey and the like who were dealing some drugs down at the beach. Yeah, those were bad kids," he said, nodding to himself. "I had that informant, Steve C., but we all called him Beaver. He knew all about Lisa," Fields said, stuttering a little at the end, out of breath from this burst of energy. Fields's companion back near the door made an impatient gesture.

"But the fire? My parents, Frank and Nancy Overton, they died," I said, shakily trying to get him to focus.

"Nah. I don't remember any fire," he spoke to his hands again. "Maybe you could talk to the county prosecutor or maybe Jimmy Barber. He's city manager of Brigantine now, but he used to be with the county prosecutor's office."

Fields threw out a few more names, and I scrambled to take notes. He was apologetic that he could not remember more. I felt strangely embarrassed, like I was trying not to look at an old man caught naked on the bus.

I nodded. The companion laid his hand on Fields's shoulder. I thanked him for his time, I think, but I was not paying much attention to my own words. I had flown three thousand miles for this meeting. I was dressed in my best—cream-colored silk and pearls and four-inch heels. I was sure the meeting would end with answers, but instead I was left sitting alone at a cheap folding table, staring at a crooked accordion wall that seemed to have run off its tracks.

I rode the elevator alone to my hotel room. There, darkness approaching, I gazed blankly at the flat city with its jutting towers of casino light. *What I need is a plan*, I thought. It's not the end. It couldn't be.

I thought about going for a run, but instead put on fresh lipstick and went back downstairs to an informal reception for the narcotics officers' meeting. Over the next few hours, some friendly detectives bought drinks for me at the hotel bar. They all claimed to have special expertise in cold cases and, if I were going to be in town for a while, they would be happy to talk more. I collected business cards and phone numbers, promising to call when I got home to California. There were so many of them willing to help. I was once again convinced that it was only a matter of time. With a little more digging, the inevitable truth would be clear.

Later that night in my room, a glass of wine on the table and supplementary investigation reports littering my hotel bed, I picked up the mystery memo. I read again that the respected Investigator Buzby called to say he was about to blow the case wide open. In the next day or two, detectives reinterviewed Lisa and Beth. Then they talked to Joey C.

Joey C., thirteen years old, a casual friend of Lisa's, was becoming the prime suspect when he walked into the police station on July 17, 1974, accompanied by his father and grandmother for an interview. Together, they faced the two main investigators and Fields's boss, Sergeant O'Brien.

> Rutley: What do you know about the Overton fire?
>
> Joey: I only know what I heard, the day after it happened. I was out of town.
>
> Sgt. O'Brien: Where were you?
>
> Joey: I was with my friends, the Trusdales. They took me to the horse races and I slept over.
>
> Rutley: Did Lisa talk to you about setting a fire, or anything about a fire? Think before you answer, did she mention anything at all about a fire?
>
> Joey: No, she did not say anything about a fire. I did see her about a week after the fire, up on Ventnor Ave. and I asked her how it started and she said she didn't know and she started to cry. Then we went to Sacco's Sub Shop and we got a sub and ate it there.

In the notes on the interview, Sergeant O'Brien wrote, "The father was a little perturbed and appeared to have a chip on his shoulder. He stated that wherever he moves to, trouble seems to follow."

And just for the record, O'Brien noted the horse races were over by midnight and the Overton fire started three hours later. The Trusdales lived about a half-mile from the Waterview townhomes.

They seemed to be developing a case at this point, getting new leads and pinning people down. So why did it take nearly two weeks for the investigators to check out Joey's story?

On July 29, when Fields and Rutley finally went to the Trusdales' house, it had been more than a month after my parents were killed. Mr. Trusdale vaguely remembered the night of the fire. Joey went to the races with them and stayed the night, Mr. Trusdale said. He didn't leave till morning. Mr. Trusdale remembered another night when Joey came over to borrow a sleeping bag because, Joey said, he preferred sleeping out in the back of his house. Maybe that chip on his dad's shoulder made it safer for Joey to sleep outside.

After visiting the Trusdales, Fields and Rutley went back to Joey's house. This time, they told Joey's parents they had information proving that Lisa Overton asked Joey to start a fire. What happened next wasn't entirely clear. Fields stiffly reported that Joey's parents "were under the impression their son was being accused of starting the fire." After that, I thought the investigators were invited to leave. Joey wasn't home, anyway.

Finally that evening, Fields and Rutley interviewed Linda O. and her mother. Linda was sixteen and Leslie's friend. The investigators had information, they told her, that Leslie called the morning after the fire and said, "We're free now; they're both dead."

Linda said *no*, according to the police report. Leslie didn't say anything like that, Linda said. Leslie called the morning after the fire and said her parents were dead. It sounded like Leslie was crying, Linda said.

Linda did agree with her mother that all of the Overton girls seemed to pass off their parents' death too lightly. They could do as they pleased, Linda said, now that their parents were gone. It seemed like they got what they wanted.

Somewhere around the end of that July, investigators Fields and Rutley requested that Lisa take a polygraph test. Marvin Perskie, the criminal defense attorney hired by Maurie Cole, politely declined on her behalf. Then, there was nothing. By mid-August, there would be no more entries in the file.

The day after my disheartening meeting with Detective Fields at the Trump Tower in Atlantic City, I lay awake half the night wondering why Detective Fields remembered a teenage girl, but not the fire that killed her parents. Fields investigated the fire at the Waterview townhomes, for heaven's sake, but claimed to remember nothing about it. But my pot-smoking, pill-selling, fourteen-year-old sister? Sure, he remembered Lisa. It didn't feel right. I was not sure if he's hiding something or if I had made a terrible mistake by approaching him at all.

What I did know was that Fields was a dead end for now, unless I was interested in hearing about his health issues in greater detail. So I grabbed at the one real straw he offered: a single name and a place where I could find the man who knew everyone.

Jimmy Barber used to be an investigator with the Atlantic County Prosecutor's Office, major crimes division. He started working there three years after my parents were killed. Now, he's city manager of Brigantine. Fields said Jimmy Barber would help me if he could. So I was back sitting in front of a New Jersey local official with my file full of precious, scavenged records balanced on my knees, hopeful. I saw light in his eyes as I finished my tale of fire and death from forty years earlier. I felt better just looking at him, sitting behind his deep wooden desk in the Brigantine City Hall, hands folded on his desk. His eyes were steady on me as I talked, but I could see the wheels turning. He knew how paper and authority flew through a bureaucracy; he could tell me where to look, whom to trust.

"Was anyone arrested?" Jimmy asked.

"No, but there was a suspect. Or maybe you would call her a person of interest," I answered. "My sister, Lisa."

Jimmy's eyebrows shot up a little, and he made a face somewhere in between sympathy and insinuation. He asked, "How old was your sister at the time?"

"She was fourteen. But Lisa was already into drugs and was stealing pills from my mother and selling them to her friends."

"Uh-huh."

"Detective Fields came to our house on a number of occasions and was getting ready to arrest her for her drug activities. She was involved with some very bad people," I said, talking fast and holding steady on Jimmy's eyes so he would know that I was okay. Whatever way the chips fell, whoever turned out to be guilty, I wanted him to know that I was determined to see this through. "There was talk that Lisa convinced some of her friends to start the fire. Or maybe she pissed off some other drug dealers."

Jimmy nodded, making notes on a pad of paper on the desk, leaning forward now, looking like a man who had fallen back into a familiar pattern and still felt the old rhythms moving in his veins. "Did her friends get interviewed?"

"They did," I said, setting the file on his desk. "There are interviews in here with several of the boys who were hanging around that night. The neighbors heard them in the parking lot."

"Okay, well, maybe I could get a copy of your file here and take a look," he said, flipping open the yellow cover and riffling idly through the forty odd pages. "I can't promise you anything, but I could look."

"Absolutely. I'd be happy to make a copy. Thank you so much," I said, feeling like I was finally getting somewhere and like I had known Jimmy Barber my whole life.

Back home in California, I read through my notes again from the Detective Fields interview and called Jimmy Barber back. Over that summer, we traded a few phone calls, and Jimmy turned out to be very sympathetic. He made some inquiries into my case, he said, and discovered that my parents were not on the homicide list for 1974. The fire was considered "suspicious" in origin, and the investigation was still open, but nobody was sure about anything back then, he reported. Also, Jimmy recognized a couple of the witness names from the file. Two of Lisa's friends who were questioned after the fire—Beth A. and Bobby M.—were still locals, Jimmy said, so he called them.

For a moment, I was breathless with gratitude that Jimmy Barber would be willing to run down leads after all this time. Before real hope could bloom, though, Jimmy sighed hard. "Guess we shouldn't be surprised that after all this time, they don't remember much. Both of them say they don't know who started the fire, just like they said at the time. Neither one of them has any new information."

We talked a little more after that about who else might have information and which agencies might have been involved. Jimmy said I should definitely talk to Chuck DeFebbo, an investigator with the Atlantic County Prosecutor's Office. They never worked together, but he'd heard good things about DeFebbo, Jimmy said.

Before I could find DeFebbo, Lisa did. On her annual summer trip back to Brigantine—this time armed with a copy of the investigative reports I gave her—she interviewed Chuck DeFebbo in person.

"You need to talk to him," Lisa wrote in an email. "He's waiting for your call."

I suspected that DeFebbo was already on Lisa's team, but I traded phone messages with him for a few weeks until August, when I finally caught him in his office.

"Sure, sure. I know who you are. I met your sister here in, let me see, June?" DeFebbo said. "Yeah. July, maybe. What can I do for you?"

I resisted saying "Tell me who killed my parents," because I thought that would seem rude. We stumbled through a few preliminaries, and he assured me that he read the same file that I had. The prosecutor's office had its own file on the case, of course, but it was destroyed in a flood in an off-site records holding facility sometime in the 1980s, he said. What he did have was a copy of the Ventnor City Police file, like I did, plus a few photographs that had been scavenged after the flood.

"I've laid everything out; and, just the way that the accelerant was on the floor, the way the fire was set up, I can tell you that nothing indicates that Lisa would have done that," DeFebbo said. "The evidence just doesn't support it."

For a moment, I was speechless. This investigator met Lisa once, and he was prepared to exonerate her completely? Obviously, he knew nothing of her previous trouble with the police.

"I know that Lisa was a bit of a hellion back then. She told me all about it," DeFebbo said, a chuckle tickling the edge of his voice. "And I have to tell you she sounds like a pretty typical teenager. Growing up, I'm afraid my friends and I were up to the same kind of stunts."

Stunts? I didn't want to be impolite, but I couldn't believe an officer of the law would pass off drug dealing as a youthful stunt. Surely, he at least understood that Lisa was attempting to manipulate him and the situation, I thought.

"You know," I said leadingly, "Lisa is very intelligent."

"Oh, she spoke very highly of you too," DeFebbo said. He went on to mention her education, her Navy service. On the pad of paper in front of me, I doodled right over DeFebbo's name and reshuffled, once again, my stack of reports.

2011

Lisa Did It, according to Jill and Doug

Guardians are necessary for children and
abnormal adults because they cannot make
responsible choices for themselves.

—Tom G. Palmer

Doug and Jill Auburn, circa 1977

After Detective Fields was struck with amnesia in the Trump Hotel
and Casino, I turned back to my family, to the people who were

adults when the fire happened. My mother's sister, Jill, and her husband, Doug, left New Jersey in the late 1990s, following their only daughter, Kim, south to Florida, land of sunshine and retirees.

They had heart trouble and aching bones, the usual complaints of old age. Aunt Jill quit drinking forty years earlier. I wanted to talk to her about Mom, but her sister was still a sore subject.

My aunt and uncle were careful with their words. They knew the fire was arson, they said, but did not know who set it. There were four girls who got out that night, and it could have been any one of us. Jill and Doug didn't like to point fingers at their nieces. In truth though, everyone knew they thought Lisa did it. They had not spoken to her in three decades.

Uncle Doug had the big, warm voice of the schoolteacher he was, and Aunt Jill still had the long New Jersey vowels even though they retired to Florida years ago. Tremors of grief crept in around the edges of their words when they talked about Nancy and Frank. I envied them for that. Their grief was not filtered by resentment or bitterness. They could mourn my parents without tripping over the facts of those last few years.

For Jill and Doug, my mother was still young and vivacious. Nancy was the center of every party, they liked to say. And Frank was a brick. He was good with his hands and a pleasant company. Sure, there had been some sibling rivalry when Jill and Nancy were young, and Nancy had an unpredictable temper; but by the time everyone was raising families together and living just a few feet apart, they learned to appreciate each other.

"We've been asking ourselves what went wrong after they moved south to Brigantine," Doug said. "I find it so hard to believe. Nancy was such a bright lady and very talented. You give her some material and a sewing machine, and she could make anything. She sewed Frank a sport coat, and you could never tell it didn't come from a store. She made Jill's wedding dress, for heaven's sake."

The few times Jill and Doug made the journey to Brigantine, we were on our best behavior. Visits to the house on 29th Street were short and picture-perfect, as if we had been rehearsing for weeks. They knew that Nancy had tried to commit suicide, but they didn't dwell on it. She seemed better. And maybe all those pills were just a temporary expression of Mom's excessive personality.

So they did not know much of what happened in my family for those nine years leading up to the fire. They just knew that they drove down from Fords the day after my parents died, prepared to make good on the promise Doug made to my dad all those years ago while looking over the dark water at Perth Amboy. Still reeling from shock, their only thought was to gather us up and take us home to Fords.

Their first hint that things were not entirely right came quickly, Jill remembered. They went to look at the town house in Ventnor Heights, a blackened ruin, and heard neighbors talking about those Overton girls. The girls didn't behave the way everyone thought they should; they were cutting up and telling jokes while the house burned down. Someone heard the girls saying they were free now. Jill's voice still registered shock, all the years later.

John and Betsy Rogge tried to prepare my aunt and uncle for the behavior problems ahead. Betsy told them to go have a talk with Lisa's middle school principal, so they would know what they were getting into. Doug demurred, so Betsy tried again. "Please go talk to the principal," Betsy said, "so you can be prepared."

"I didn't go," Doug said flatly. "My thought was no matter what they would say, I was going to have Lisa in my house. We weren't going to pick and choose which girl would come home with us. That wasn't the promise we made."

Jill and Doug went home after the funeral and started preparing for my sisters' arrival. They took some money from my cousin Kim's college fund and added two bedrooms and a bathroom to their house. The whole place was a construction zone that summer while my sisters and I were staying with the Rogges.

"And then one day, I got a call from the police in Ventnor wanting to know if it was okay to give Lisa a lie detector test," Aunt Jill said. "I said, 'Wait a minute. I need to think about that.' When Doug got home that day, we talked about it, and then I remembered I had a friend from high school who was now sheriff of Middlesex County. I thought he could help us find someone to administer the test up in

Fords first, just so we would know what we were dealing with. My friend said he was real sorry, but he couldn't help us. He said that was an Atlantic City case. He didn't want to mess with that. I guess, with all those powerful people involved, he thought it wouldn't be so good for his career." For Aunt Jill, it was another sign that things were out of her control.

Lisa had told me that the defense attorneys, who also wanted to know what they might be dealing with, arranged for her to take a polygraph that summer before she left Brigantine. Apparently, this was done without Aunt Jill's consent. Maybe that's acceptable if a defense attorney ordered it. Lisa's memory of the test was sketchy, but she told me she was overcome with emotion and failed the test. The examiner asked if she set the fire, her voice quavered badly when she said "no," and that was it. Nobody really looked at her after that. Now that I thought about it, that might have been the only time that anyone ever directly asked that question of Lisa. The police and fire investigators never did, based on their reports and transcripts. It had been hoped that the lie detector test would clear Lisa, but instead, it only served to fuel people's suspicions.

I did not know if Jill and Doug knew about the failed polygraph test when Lisa arrived to Fords, curtly dropped off by the Rogges after running away. But for a couple of weeks, everything was all right. Lisa minded them well enough and was quiet.

Then, Leslie and Liz arrived, and the house was filled with noise and activity and hungry, growing teenagers. Every week, Jill found herself shopping for more groceries. As she arrived home with brown paper bags stuffed with boxes of sugary sweet cereal, English muffins, cartons of orange and apple juice, and whole milk, my sisters met her on the porch, rushed to the car, and offered to help carry the bags into the house. At first, Jill was impressed at how helpful they were, until she realized their true motive. They set the groceries on the kitchen table, "and the girls would just fall on them, tearing into the bags like they had been in a prisoner of war camp or something," Jill said. "I'd never seen anything like it."

Once, Uncle Doug came into the living room to find a bunch of teenaged girls—his nieces—lying on their bellies, propped up by pillows, watching cartoons in their t-shirts and panties. I thought he must have reeled, temporarily blinded by the scantily clad bodies, and quickly retreated from the room. He informed my sisters, "Hey, I have a ten-year-old boy living here. You can't lie around like that." It was one of the only times, Doug said, that the girls acquiesced without backtalk. They fled to their bedrooms and returned properly covered in pajama bottoms and robes.

After school started and Lisa made some new friends, hopes for a quiet integration of the two families evaporated. Lisa soon had a new boyfriend, and my sisters made new drug connections. Doug remembered walking in on Leslie "rolling a smoke" in the girls' basement bedroom. He asked what she was doing; and, always the cool one, Leslie shrugged and told him it was oregano—like he was going to believe that.

Lisa blew her curfew more than once. The way Lisa told the story now, Aunt Jill was shaky with a hangover one morning and fortifying her morning coffee from a bottle when she remarked that "You're a slut, just like your mother." Lisa lunged at her. There was a struggle, and then Lisa took off again. She went to live at her new boyfriend's house, and it took Uncle Doug a week to track her down. He explained to the boy's father—an adult for chrissakes—that Lisa had a legal guardian and she could not decide, at fourteen, to live wherever she wanted. After a few more reminders about the law and what was right, Doug left, and Lisa returned home to them. A couple of days later, a neighbor saw that same boy sticking an ice pick into the tires on Doug's car.

Uncle Doug said, "Lisa's favorite word was the 'F' word. I would take her aside and say, 'I am not going to tolerate this. I have my own children here, and we don't have this kind of emotional breakdowns in this house.' Everything was a blowup."

At night, away from the kids, Jill and Doug speculated on what had happened to Nancy and Frank down south. How had everything gone so badly? They were becoming more vigilant. Every time Jill and Doug went out to a movie or to see friends for dinner, Doug wedged a wooden match between the back door and the doorframe so he would know if the girls snuck out against his wishes, he said. He had seen this trick in a movie once. Almost every time, that match would be on the ground.

Uncle Doug, who taught psychology at a nearby high school, sent Lisa to a psychologist. But Lisa only had two sessions before the therapist dropped her. Or maybe it was Lisa who quit. With Jill and Doug both working full-time and taking care of four other kids, there was no time to find another psychologist for an unwilling teenager.

Maybe Jill and Doug could have been more empathetic toward my grieving sisters, newly orphaned and acting out like unruly teenagers. But I did understand insisting on limits to the chaos.

Sometime that autumn, after school started, Jill and Doug finally got a call from someone connected to the investigation. Lisa's defense attorney, Marvin Perskie, was inviting them down to Atlantic City for a chat, Doug remembered.

Now, Perskie had been hired to represent Lisa in a possible criminal case, but it never seemed like he was working for our family. Instead, he was a voice of authority. Perskie had been a state assemblyman; he was the son of a state Supreme Court justice, and his family was in the news a lot that year as the Perskies were a driving force behind the proposal to bring casino gambling to Atlantic City. It was all anyone was talking about.

Jill and Doug told me they made the two-hour drive down to Atlantic City to find themselves at a table with Marvin Perskie, the tall and well-connected attorney, Maurie Cole, and Mayor John Rogge. I tried to imagine that meeting and wondered if John Rogge traded notes with my aunt and uncle on the Overton girls or exchanged stiff "hellos" from me to my sisters and back. Already, there was a gulf between us that was wider than the actual one hundred miles of Garden State Parkway between Brigantine and Fords. I belonged to the Rogges, and my sisters belonged to Jill and Doug; I was content with that and hoped nothing would change.

No, there probably wasn't much social banter. Jill and Doug felt outmatched from the beginning; and besides, Uncle Doug said, the men did not call the meeting to consult. They were there to inform.

"It was clear within a few minutes they were not going to pursue any investigation into the arson, and they didn't want us to either.

They said it would be hurtful to the girls," Doug recalled, a rare bitterness creeping into his voice. "These girls were so young, they said; and even if Lisa did set the fire, all that would happen was she would go to a reformatory for a few years. What good would a reformatory do? We didn't think it was right, but what could we do?"

After talking with Jill and Doug during those months, it was easy to see how powerful forces could have shut down the arson investigation. Maybe it wasn't a backroom cabal, exactly, with shadowy power brokers blocking investigators. It was good-hearted men, trying to avoid a scandal and get double indemnity for those four orphaned girls. I thought about these lawyers telling investigators— telling the elected Atlantic County prosecutor—that the family just wasn't going to cooperate and would not assist the investigation. It would be easier, wouldn't it, to press on to more solvable cases? Fire leaves a trail that is open to so many interpretations. And by this time, the trail had grown cold.

Doug and Jill returned home to Fords and wrestled with the new tenor of their home. Liz was quiet and kept to herself, but Leslie and Lisa were constantly getting into new trouble. And Lisa was brazen. For the first time in Jill's life, she remembered, police officers were coming to the house talking to her about vandalism and drugs and the kids in her house. She and Doug tried to shield their own kids, Kim and Ross, from the turbulence; but it wasn't getting better. They found a few burned matches lying around—in a medicine cabinet or in the bottom of a paper grocery sack. They began to worry more.

Doug asked the contractor working on the addition to his house to cut another door in the wall, from the master bedroom to the outside—just in case. Months went by like this.

Lisa's side of the end-game story went like this: She was hanging out in the girls' restroom at the junior high school toward the end of her ninth grade year. Someone showed her how you could hold a lit match or lighter to an edge of the toilet seat and it would ignite in a ring of fire. It was a lot cooler than throwing lumps of wet toilet tissue onto the ceiling to make them stick. She wasn't stupid about it. Lisa studied the bathroom's tile floors, metal doors, and porcelain toilets and decided it would not catch fire. So she lit the toilet seat and got caught.

I guess it did not occur to Lisa that the girl suspected of setting the fire that killed her parents should not be setting fires in the girls' restroom. It occurred to everyone else, though. She was suspended from school. Doug and Jill threw up their hands too, and she was taken into custody at Middlesex County Juvenile Detention; and after a court hearing the next day, she was placed at Menlo Park Diagnostic Center about five miles from Fords. Lisa was charged with arson and incorrigibility, and nobody felt safe around her.

Jill and Doug remembered visiting her a couple of times. They brought her things she needed, and she seemed calmer. Lisa was put into a special program for gifted, troubled teens, Jill remembered, and one day a director with the program called to say they were taking the kids on a day trip to New York City as a special treat. Jill told them, "I wouldn't do that. She will run for sure. You do not know how smart that girl is."

In the retelling, Jill threw up her hands all over again. "Sure enough, they called me about a week later and asked did I know where Lisa was. Can you believe it?"

Lisa said that only Doug visited once, bringing all her belongings in three green trash bags. She was never in a special program, Lisa said, and never went to New York. The official record lacked detail. While at Menlo Park Diagnostic Center, however, Lisa admitted that she stole the matron's keys and ran off with three other kids. It wasn't even that hard, she said.

"So someone from the state called me and wanted me to pay to have all the locks replaced in this facility," Doug said. "I told them, 'You're crazy! I'm not the one that let her get away.' We warned them about her."

After Lisa escaped from the diagnostic center, Jill came home to find the back window broken. The only things missing from the house belonged to Lisa. Later, Jill heard that Lisa was telling people that her aunt was keeping things from her and that she had to break in to get her stuff.

"Nancy was *my* sister," Aunt Jill said. The sentence began fiercely, but then her voice cracked. "We didn't get along well as kids, but she was my sister. And I'll tell you something—until they prove that someone else set that fire, I'm not trusting Lisa."

At the end of that traumatic year after the fire, with their house in turmoil and desperation to protect their own children, Jill and Doug relinquished custody of Lisa. By this time, Leslie—who had always been Lisa's closest ally—had her doubts about Lisa's innocence. She never believed that Lisa lit the match, but she was starting to think that Lisa knew more about what happened than she was admitting. It must have been uncomfortable, living in that household.

Lisa spent the summer of 1975 in juvenile detention and the county shelter and somehow talked the authorities into allowing her to go live with her friend Beth's family. The family agreed to take Lisa on the condition that she attend Holy Spirit, the local Catholic high school. But when she was kicked out for behavior problems, she went off to live with a boyfriend. At some point, she was taken into custody for being a runaway, but she convinced the court to award guardianship of her to Leslie, who had turned eighteen a few months earlier.

Later, she attempted suicide with a bunch of pills. She was sixteen. From the regular hospital, Lisa was transported to Fair Oaks Psychiatric Hospital in Summit, where she was committed with Leslie's consent. On the advice of adults, Leslie gave up guardianship, and Lisa returned to the revolving door of juvenile detention and psychiatric facilities that could be the life of a runaway. A year and a half later she turned 18 and, like the rest of us, she collected her inheritance money.

Uncle Doug told me now that he wished he had suffered through the inevitable histrionics from my sisters and withheld their inheritance until the age of twenty-five. But he was tired of fighting.

When I became an adult, nine months after my parents were killed, I got a big check. The Rogges invited a financial advisor friend over who helped me invest in a mix of blue-chip stocks where my money could grow. Interest and dividends helped me pay my way through college, along with my part-time job at the local flower shop. The principal balance would eventually provide my husband and me with a down payment for our house in California.

Leslie got her money when she turned eighteen, a few months before high school graduation. I thought Uncle Doug must have handed her a check and then covered his eyes. Leslie bought a fancy leather jacket and a brown Camaro which had a clutch that needed to be replaced every few months. She couldn't get out of Fords quickly enough. She moved in with Lisa in Atlantic City and graduated from high school there a few months later. She was carefree in those years and seemed to have a lot of fun. Sometimes, I was jealous.

Lisa told me that she blew her inheritance in a year. She became a heroin addict and sometime thief. I saw her rarely. It would be wrong to write Lisa off, however. Even though she was a full-blown addict, she managed to earn her bachelor's degree in criminal justice from Stockton State College, just like mine. I thought she even made the honor roll. I didn't think I ever asked Lisa why she chose that field. I studied criminal justice because I wanted to be a lawyer and I was told that this was a good prelaw field of study. Why Lisa chose it as well was a testament to how thoroughly we were still captivated by the criminal case nobody ever discussed.

Liz fell for a guy who was good with cars, and she used her money to help him buy a gas station. It didn't work out for long. She continued to stay in Fords and live with Jill and Doug until she went to college.

It's funny how all of us sisters had drifted apart and back together through the years, like magnets in a dish that keep switching polarity. Leslie got pregnant, went to California, fell in love with the place, and wrote glowing letters to all of us about the sunshine in Chino. She gave birth to a daughter and set about raising her alone.

After visiting Leslie, Lisa decided to move to California too. After a twenty-eight-day drug rehab, she finagled an entry-level job in the newsroom of a local paper. But an accident involving all-terrain vehicles in the desert and the painkillers prescribed for her injuries sent Lisa reeling back into active addiction within months. She was arrested and briefly jailed on a felony cocaine possession charge and fled back to New Jersey before the trial, where Uncle John—who did not know about the pending criminal charge—helped her enlist into the Navy. Two weeks short of six years later, Lisa left the Navy with a medical discharge and remained in California for another fresh start. Along the way, she married and divorced twice, got clean and sober, raised two daughters mostly on her own, and became a volunteer counselor for recovering addicts.

I took the more traditional route. After getting married in New Jersey to my long-time boyfriend, Jeff, we struck out for California where Jeff's family had jobs waiting for us. I stepped off the plane in San Francisco and knew immediately and with every fiber of my being that I found home. Jeff and I settled in the Bay Area and had two children. When my first child, Drew, was born, Liz moved from New Jersey to live with us and take care of the baby. She stayed for two years before moving out on her own.

Somehow, decades went by as we Overton girls raised our children. Leslie and her daughter lived with us for a while too, when my son became sick with Duchenne muscular dystrophy (DMD). Drew died at the age of twelve, and my sisters stood beside me as we scattered his ashes in the golden hills of a park near my home. We gathered on holidays and on birthdays, and we never talked about the fire. It is a tribute, I suppose, to what it means to be a sister, to be blood related. Even if I thought my sister might have done something unspeakably horrible, I did not turn away from her.

In these pages, among all the pieces of paper that bear the names of Lisa and me, there is one that haunts my conscience: a notice to appear regarding custody of Lisa Overton, a minor. I was nineteen, living with the Rogges and attending college. I could remember Betsy shaking her head slowly, firmly. "Don't do it," Betsy said, handing back my court paperwork. "You're just now pulling your life together. Lisa is trouble."

Or maybe she said, "Lisa is troubled." Either way, everyone I talked to said the same thing: Don't get involved. They told me to focus on my own life. So I told the lawyer *no*, and I didn't think I was ever called in to that hearing. I just waited outside, sitting with my ankles crossed, dreading the sight of my sister. That was when Leslie was awarded custody, keeping Lisa out of juvenile detention.

Remembering that moment, I was washed in regret. My sister, an orphan like me in those first raw years of our grief, was bounced around to so many institutions and families and hospitals; and everyone turned her away. One minute, she was rebelling against Mom even while knowing she was Mom's favorite daughter. Then Mom and Dad were dead, and people were whispering behind her back. Then Lisa was sixteen, sad and alone, and nobody wanted her— nobody. A soft, hiccupping sob hit me square in the chest. It was difficult to even imagine the vast, harsh loneliness this was for her. If this had happened to me, what would I have become?

2012

THE SISTERS' MEETING

Children begin by loving their parents;
as they grow older they judge them;
sometimes they forgive them.

—Oscar Wilde

Leigh, Liz, Les, Jessica, Lisa, Leah, Larissa,
and Maria (front row); April 2012

By the time my sisters and our daughters gathered in April 2012 in the living room area of our suite at the Residence Inn in Oxnard, California, they knew what the meeting was about. But I stood in front of the kitchenette, hands on the back of a sofa, and addressed the room anyway.

"I think you guys know that I'm working on a book about us, about growing up and the fire," I began. I scanned the faces in the room but skimmed over the eyes. I needed my sisters, and that need made me feel a little panicky.

Over the past eighteen months since my meeting with Detective Fields, I had written and rewritten the same pages, obsessing over every nuance in the interviews between our teenage selves and investigators who were long dead or living with dementia in nursing homes. I kept running into dead ends.

"We've had the fire investigation reports and police files for more than three years now, and we still don't know a whole lot more than we did. So I'm asking for your help," I continued. "This is my story, my memories. But there are some things I can't quite pull together."

I was sure that Liz, restless and pacing, did not want to talk about the fire. I was surprised she was there at all. I kept expecting her to retreat into one of the bedrooms any moment and close the door. Liz was always the sensitive, quiet one. She moved west when I had my first baby and lived with us for a year, caring for my son, playing endless hours of games, and reading to him. I was still sorry she never had children of her own because she would have made a great mom. Now she looked a bit disheveled and agitated. With that sweat suit she was wearing, she looked as though she hadn't made her plan for the day. Since she was laid off from her job with a large financial firm two years ago, she'd only had part-time work as a notary public. It sometimes seemed like she was disappearing right before my eyes, going blurry around the edges.

Lisa was in an easy chair in the furthest corner from me, beside a large window filled with a big blue sky crossed with a few high clouds. She kept moving in and out of focus for me. A strong ray of sunlight lit up the dust motes between us and screened her from view, but then a cloud would cover the sun, and she would reappear from the shadow. Lisa still had the firm, square jaw of her youth, and living in San Diego gave her a year-round tan. The highlights in her wavy cropped hair were now silver over gray, reminding me that we were all past fifty. Lisa's hands lay one within the other on her lap, and she watched me without expression.

Leslie was sitting on the other side of the window, barely contained within her skin. She was still a quick talker and full of energy. From an easy-going, not-very-confident girlhood, Leslie had grown into a capable woman. She raised a daughter alone, learned how to use tools, and could still fix just about anything. A pile of splinters and broken glass could turn into a completely functional and cozy home in her hands. She fought and won battles with alcohol and cigarettes and excess weight, and I was so proud of her strength and grace, even if she could be a bit cranky sometimes. Like her, I too wished she could have the occasional glass of wine. It would substantially improve her mood.

Our four daughters sat on a love seat facing Leslie and Lisa across a faux wood coffee table. Looking at them lined up and waiting, I felt a flash of pride. These girls were healthy and happy, proof that we had drawn a line and kept the damage from infecting the next generation. I knew that my sisters and I had sacrificed relationships and personal dreams for the sake of our children—something our own mother never did. We might have five failed marriages between us; but the bad mothering cycle, at least, had been broken.

Of course, I worried that Lisa's two teenagers were too young for this conversation. But I was not about to question Lisa's judgment. They remained seated on the love seat facing their mother, while my daughter, Jessica, sat a little to one side, turning her chair so she could see the entire room. Leslie's daughter, Leah, who married last year, rocked back and forth in her chair searching for a more comfortable position for her big round belly. Leah was due to give birth in a few weeks, and it was for her baby shower that we gathered in this seaside town north of Los Angeles. The shower was Saturday. On Sunday morning, we were sitting on eggshells.

"For instance," I said, "I've been trying to piece together the circumstances around Mom's suicide attempts. I remember the first and the last and maybe one in the middle, but there are two or three others, and I can't remember: pills or the razor?"

What I really wanted to talk about was who started the fire, whether Lisa and Leslie had suspicions. We had never speculated together on who the arsonist might be, so I led with the suicide attempts as a kind of warm-up. It seemed ghoulish now that I'd said it.

Leslie spoke up first, "I remember the first one. August 14, 1966," she said in a quick, staccato delivery as if she had been repeating the story for years. "It was a Sunday like any other Sunday except Mom went to church. Mom never went to church. Leigh and I were singing in the choir. We went with her. We got donuts on the way home. We never got donuts. Later, we were all at the beach when Mom came down and fell asleep on a blanket. We couldn't wake her up, and the tide was coming in."

We each had our own version of this story, of course, but fell into stunned silence, listening to Leslie. It's like every word was being fired from her mouth. Maybe she was afraid of being interrupted.

"Later, Mom wrote me a letter saying that I had to be a very good girl because she was sick and had problems and had to stay in the hospital," Leslie said.

"I don't remember getting any letters from Mom," I said.

"Well, I probably wrote to her first," Leslie said.

"Of course," I said. "That makes sense."

The suicide attempt that Lisa remembered best, she said, was the day after Grandmom's funeral. She had all sorts of details that I did not.

"Do you remember the funeral?" Lisa said. Even as an adult, her voice had a light girlishness to it; words were pronounced with a roundness, and a slight lisp softened the sharp edges. "Grandmom looked so terribly fake we couldn't stop laughing."

"Oh, God. Mom was completely wasted on the drive to the cemetery. Dad had to hold her up," Leslie said.

"That night, Mom came into Gram's room where Liz and I were sleeping and turned on the light," Lisa said. "She was wearing that old red robe that she made. She had a dishtowel wrapped around her wrist. I said, 'What's that?' She said, 'I'm going off to join your grandmother.' She started unwrapping the towel, and it was all red."

"Oh my god. She came into my room first," Leslie said, nearly shouting over the buzzing voices in the room. "She woke me up and said, 'See what I did?' I said 'So what?' and rolled over. I was fifteen. I didn't care."

Lisa told of waking up Dad and how he said, "Shit, Nance, couldn't you wait another day?" Then we started counting the suicide attempts.

There was the first one, on the beach. There was the Thanksgiving episode in Fords, when Aunt Jill was making dinner at her house and Mom was jealous so she stayed in bed and took a bunch of pills. There was another attempt one spring, between my birthday and Leslie's. We thought it was a razor that time. Grandmom's funeral and the bloody bed episode were just a few weeks before the fire rounded out the list.

"So wait. We've got three razors, two pills?" Leslie asked in all seriousness, but somehow that sent all of us into gales of laughter.

Lisa was still chuckling a little and wiping at one eye when she said, "I just remember May 1, 1974, coming home from school that day."

"I was babysitting," Leslie interrupted. "You called me and said, 'Les, don't panic. Mom tried to kill herself again.' There was blood everywhere. I know that Atlantic County officials told Dad that if there were any more suicide attempts, they were going to step in, disband the family, and put Mom away for good."

This was the first I heard about county officials threatening to disband our family, but I was not surprised. Over these past three years spent digging through dusty papers and watching home movies, I began to remember all sorts of details that adulthood suppressed. For instance, Dad told me a day or two before the fire that he might have to give up Leslie and Lisa to the authorities. He said they were incorrigible and making Mom's condition worse.

I realized now this might not have been his idea. Maybe Dad was trying to outmaneuver the county, shedding the bad seeds to save the remaining family. Or maybe Dad thought their rebelliousness was the cause of Mom's suicide attempts. If Lisa and Leslie were out of the picture, Dad might have thought Mom would be cured. It was chilling to think of my dad calculating like that. He was willing to turn out two teenage daughters, it seemed. What else would he throw out?

"And then how about the time Mom left me in Tandy Leather?" Liz was saying, loud and flat.

I'd been dimly aware of Liz walking circles at one end of the room near a bedroom door and muttering. Occasionally, she would bark out some half-joking comment like "What donuts? I didn't get any donuts."

This time, Liz was unyielding. Yesterday, she swore that I could not make her talk about the fire or Mom or any of this. Now, she was demanding to be heard and pointing herself at Lisa.

"You were supposed to go," Liz was not crying, but her voice trembled. "I tried to bribe you with Tastykakes."

It was just the two youngest girls at home on the day Mom realized she had run out of leather and needed to make a run to Philadelphia. Mom was teaching arts and crafts that summer to the neighborhood kids in the community center of the Waterview townhomes. She was busy. She had found a friend nearby, and she was taking responsibility for certain aspects of daily life, like showing up to teach those classes and occasionally paying attention to how we were spending our last days of freedom before school started again.

Still, Liz did not like being alone with Mom, especially with a car involved. None of us willingly got into the car with Mom since the day she picked us up from school in Brigantine and then lurched out into traffic, slurring that we were on our way to see Grandmom.

I was sitting in the front seat next to Mom, holding tight to the passenger door. I could see she had a flask in her lap and her lipstick was smeared. Mom was nodding slowly to herself and couldn't stay in her lane for the length of an entire block.

"Whoa," Lisa said from the back seat.

"Let's pull over," I said. "Just for a minute."

"Mom," Leslie yelped as the car swerved sharply. "What are you doing?"

The bridge to Atlantic City approached quickly. It wasn't a long bridge, but I thought about those low railings and the water rush-

ing deep underneath, and my stomach turned cold. Mom pulled the
steering wheel left and then right, swerving around another station
wagon, coming within an inch or two of its bumper. In the back seat,
Liz started to cry.

"Please, Mom," I said, trying for a reasonable voice. "We'll be
good. We promise."

Mom's right arm gestured wildly, and she nodded twice more
to herself, eyelids fluttering hard and then falling closed as her upper
body jerked toward the steering wheel. Someone screamed. It might
have been me, as I grabbed hold of the steering wheel and turned
us away from the lane of traffic heading to the bridge. We bounced
down an embankment, barely missed a telephone pole, and landed
hard in a ditch. Then we all scrambled out of the car, before she
could wake up and start driving again.

Years had passed since that crash. But our reluctance to get in
the car with Mom had become both ingrained and unspoken. It sank
to the level of instinct, like ducking at loud noises. So maybe Liz did
not have the words to argue that day as to why she should not go
with Mom. She stood there in front of the town house, eyeing the car
with fear. Mom came out the front door and called to Liz.

"Let's get moving," Mom said as Liz shuffled back a few steps
toward the house.

"Wait a minute," Liz said. "Just a second."

Liz ran into the kitchen where Lisa was looking through cup-
boards. "Aren't you coming with us?" Liz panted.

"No way," Lisa said, not even turning around.

"What? No, you have to," Liz said. "Mom said."

"Ha-ha. Fuck that," Lisa said. "Weren't there bananas in here?"

"I have Tastykakes," Liz said.

Lisa turned to her sharply. "You do not."

"I do. I have a chocolate one. You can have it," Liz said.

"Okay. Where is it?"

"It's in the car," Liz said, not looking at Lisa. "You can have it
all."

If Lisa paused, it was only for a split second. "No way," she said.
"I'm not going anywhere with her."

"Please?" Liz said, her voice shaking as the front door swung open.

"Liz, let's go!" Mom called out.

Lisa thrust her jaw forward, turned, and ran into the dining room, away from the front door. Liz was not bold enough to disobey.

The trip to Philadelphia took about ninety minutes; and then, off the highway, there were a few grimy city blocks to navigate before they found the store. Tandy Leather Factory shut down its Philly store years ago, but in those days, it was a pilgrimage that every crafter in the area knew by heart. For Liz, who rarely left Brigantine or Ventnor, Philadelphia must have seemed massive and filthy.

At least the store was packed with things to look at. Liz wandered up and down the aisles, fingering leather strips and decorative metal pieces while Mom gathered her supplies. Mom went to the cashier's desk, but Liz did not see whether she paid. Then Mom came breezing right past Liz, saying something about going to get the car.

"You wait right here," Mom said. "I'll get the car. Be right back."

Liz stayed perfectly still for a while, looking at her shoes, willing Mom to reappear. She waited by the big front windows looking out at the alien, narrow street, the hot and grimy afternoon. Liz parked herself by the front door for a while, eyes crawling over every car that turned the corner. She held on to a metal rail and waited.

After an hour or two, one of the clerks reached out to the eleven-year-old girl waiting by the front door with her wet cheeks. Liz said she was fine and was just waiting for her mother. Mom would come back, Liz was sure. Someone offered her a cold can of soda, and Liz gave up her vigil by the door. She wandered the aisles, inspected the packages, and read the directions on every packaged craft project in the store.

One of the clerks gave her a candy bar. Liz still insisted she was fine, of course. She would never say Mom was crazy or drunk or a lousy mother—not to an outsider. She sat on the floor down one little-used aisle, ate her candy bar, and read some more directions.

Six or eight hours after she left—well past lunch and into the fading light of a late summer evening—Mom returned, obviously drunk. "Ready to go," she slurred, forgetting to make it a question.

None of the clerks said a word nor made any attempt to stop them as Mom hustled Liz out the door.

Liz didn't remember much of the drive home, traveling east on the Atlantic City Expressway as the sun sank behind them. But she remembered arriving at the twenty-five-cent toll just before the exit to Ventnor. It was an unmanned booth, where you threw your change into a bucket and the machines knew by the weight of the coins whether you had paid enough money. Of course, Mom didn't have a quarter.

If you shorted the toll, a red flashing light alerted everyone that you were a cheat. If a patrol car was waiting nearby, you got pulled over. Liz was old enough to know that since the driver in this case was obviously drunk and out of control, bad things would happen if she was found out. Liz and Mom emptied her wallet and purse, dug through the seat cushions, and came up with twenty-four cents. Mom tossed it in the bucket and drove through, holding her breath. Liz was terrified of being pulled over, of the police discovering this terrible secret of her reckless, drunken mother at the wheel of the car, as if having her pain and fear revealed to outsiders would be worse than the pain itself.

Then Lisa started talking about Mom teaching vacation Bible school one year and how she saw Mom in the bathroom sneaking sips from a flask before going back to the classroom to teach little kids about Jesus. Leslie remembered Mom showing up drunk to parent-teacher conferences. It was horrible.

I was quiet for a while, having blocked most of this information from myself for decades. Why remember all these awful moments of shame? When Mom and Dad became tragic victims of a terrible crime, it overshadowed everything else they had been. Why dredge up their failings now?

No. I knew I needed to face them in truth if I wanted to know what happened to Mom and Dad. Watching my sisters, I could see that saying these things out loud lessened the shame a little. It was a burden we all shared instead of harboring alone.

"Do you remember how people would bring us clothes and meals?" I asked. "They would bring us stuff all the time, and nobody ever mentioned Mom."

"Sure," Leslie said. "They felt sorry for us."

"Hell, looking back on it, *I* feel sorry for us," Lisa said.

We're all quiet for a moment, but then someone brought up the money they collected for us too. The Overton Children's Fund was established after the fire; and, combined with my parents' life insurance, it paid each of us when we turned eighteen. Leslie had all the figures in her head and laid them out: Dad's life insurance was one hundred thousand dollars with a double indemnity clause for accidental death, minus their debts, added to the fund, divided four ways.

"Wait," I said. "The insurance paid as an accidental death? The reports here state that there was an accelerant used in the fire with multiple points of origin. How is that an accident?"

"All I know is that Maurie Cole got that for us. It was labeled an accident so that we could get more money," Leslie said.

"Was that why Maurie Cole and the others were so keen for Uncle Doug to agree to drop the investigation?" I asked.

"Absolutely," Lisa said.

"So we could get the money," Leslie said, nodding. "They knew nothing good was going to come of the investigation."

There's silence in the room. I wondered aloud whether, money aside, they did us a disservice by shutting down that investigation. Finally, Lisa spoke.

"In 20-20 hindsight, yeah, they did us a disservice," she said carefully. "But if I was an adult in that situation, I would have done the exact same thing. They said, 'Here are four girls whose lives have been shattered, and here's this pot of money.' If it comes to light that the people who caused this thing were themselves the arsonists and murderers, think of all the stigma and problems."

I didn't know who said it first, but then we were talking about Dad as the most likely suspect. In our minds, there were two possibilities—a stranger or one of us. Mom was incapable, I thought. She was a shambling wreck. That left a stranger or Dad. And somehow, in this moment, it was just easier to imagine Dad than a stranger.

Lisa and Leslie fell into an animated conversation about what might have triggered Dad into arson, while I held back. Dad was a possibility, sure, but I couldn't quite fully commit to the idea. Yes, he was facing the possible dissolution of his family. He was broke and had no summer job. But Dad was also a volunteer fireman, for heaven's sake. I didn't know any families that had as many fire drills as mine did.

"Anyway, the truth needs to be told," Lisa was saying to the room. She nodded at me. "The truth will out eventually, anyway. But we need to know, now. We deserve to have the truth."

With that, I felt that I had Lisa's full blessing to tell this story, and I felt a rush of gratitude. I did not even know I was waiting for her approval, but the relief I felt proved it.

"And really, let's be serious," Liz said from her corner. "If Mom and Dad had lived and we had stayed in Brigantine... Sheesh." She pointed at Lisa. "She would be in jail." Then she pointed at Leslie. "*She* would be dead," Liz said. "I would be pregnant and have eighteen children."

"And Leigh would own the other half of Brigantine," Leslie said, and we all burst out laughing again.

"And we still would have buried Mom and Dad a long time ago," I said.

Liz snorted. "No. We would be caring for them right now. Picture that." The laughter died out completely.

"The decisions that were made back then," I began and then faltered. I gathered myself and tilted into it again. I had to say these words out loud, or I would burn with them forever. "They did the best they could. Only, now I know we all want more information. We need to know what happened because to tell you the truth, Lisa, I thought you were involved somehow."

Leslie nodded quickly and said, "Yes."

"I don't think you actually started it," I said quickly trying to minimize the sting of these words.

"Yeah, I never thought you started it," Leslie said. "But I thought your friends had something to do with it."

Lisa was completely still, face raised and eyes straight ahead, not really looking at any of us. I thought I saw one of Lisa's daughters shudder a little as if crying. Leslie was forging ahead, becoming more emphatic with every word.

"I worshipped the ground you walked on, at that age," Leslie said. "But you were so angry. Lisa would say 'fuck you' to me, and I would feel lower than dirt. She had so much venom behind those words, so much anger."

Sun struck the window again, and Lisa dissolved behind the scrim of bright dust motes. Lisa's older daughter asked, "Did they really think you did that, Mom?" I was standing behind the girl so I could not see her face, but from the shake of her shoulders, I thought she was crying.

My heart felt stopped in my chest, waiting and powerless. Everyone seemed to be talking at once, and the conversation made a couple of fast turns as if we were all backing away quickly in different directions. Liz said something then about being left alone again, and suddenly, Lisa was crying.

"I'm sorry, Liz," she wailed. "I am just so sorry. For leaving you alone. For everything."

Liz said she knew. Hands made fluttering motions all around the room, as if they were patting Lisa all over.

"There was stuff that… I'm sorry," Lisa sobbed and then collected herself. "And I will say again that, as far as the fire goes, I woke up in the middle of the night and the house was on fire. I mean how could I have started that fire and then lived with myself for thirty-eight years?"

"I know. I know," I said quickly, so no one could interrupt, and then I started crying too. "I feel bad that I couldn't fix it. I couldn't make anything better back then. I was just trying to get away. I couldn't save anyone. I couldn't save myself." I dried my eyes on a tissue and then started to outline a new plan, to go back to Brigantine this summer and talk to the investigators again. "Surely," I said, "I can shake something loose now. I'm in a position in life where I can help. I want to do that, because we have a right to know what happened. We can make this right."

Leslie nodded vigorously and said, "We are all here. We're already starting to make it right."

"And you know what's funny?" I said. "I think Mom and Dad would be really proud of us."

Lisa laughed a little, but she's still crying too so it sounded a little strangled. "It is funny, but it's true. I think they would be proud."

"I need to go back to Brigantine, I think, to talk to some people and see if we can't find closure," I said. "I'm thinking about this summer."

"I'll come too," Lisa said without hesitation. "I was probably going to bring the girls anyway to see Aunt Betsy and Uncle John. Let's coordinate."

"Okay," I said, blinking away the remaining tears. "Let's go together."

1967

THE DARK SIDE OF BRIGANTINE

Now those memories come back to
haunt me; they haunt me like a curse.
—Bruce Springsteen

Church directory photo, circa 1967

In the weeks following the meeting with my sisters, I found I could no longer remember what Chanel No. 5 smelled like or feel the swoosh of Mom's full skirts brushing past. The year before, I could easily recall lying on the living room floor coloring or reading at

Dad's feet while Mom's voice and then Dad's wove together in the airspace above my head like a protective canopy.

When I thought about Dad now, other memories pushed to the front. I would start to think about the smell of his pipe tobacco, and suddenly I was eleven years old. Dad was there, waving me into the kitchen of the house in Brigantine to show me what he had done. He stood at the back door with a roll of Scotch tape in his hand. While I watched, he reached up high and stretched two strips of tape from the door to the jamb.

"See, I'm taping the door high up because nobody looks up when they open a door. They look down at the door knob," Dad told me. "So she won't know that the tape is there, but we can see if this door has been opened because the tape will be broken."

He wasn't talking about Lisa or Leslie sneaking out; he was talking about Mom. She was supposed to stay sober, but instead kept slipping out at night and walking to the Circle Tavern where sometimes the regulars would buy her drinks. Or Mom would wait until we were all asleep and walk over to Jim B.'s house. I knew about Jim too. I was the only one with a bedroom on the ground floor, and sometimes, I heard things.

Jim B. lived with his mother in a big old house kitty corner from our Cape Cod. Mrs. B owned a jewelry store in Atlantic City, and her house looked like an antebellum mansion. I was surprised to remember so clearly the shadowy interior of that house, filled with dark wood, the air thick with dust. The way his family talked about Jim, it seemed like he was a bit of a drifter, a sweet-talking fellow who lived off his mother. My mom thought he was fun. One night, she came home from his house with an aquamarine ring. It was a large square-cut gemstone in a gold setting. She said only that it was a gift from a friend. There was other expensive jewelry that she flaunted too.

I didn't think any of us really understood what was happening at the time. But when my sisters and I talked about it in the phone calls that were far more frequent in the months after our meeting, we laughed at how obvious it was—and how sordid. In the letters between my mom and grandmom, it's quickly apparent my mom was fooling nobody but us kids:

> Dawn comes much later these days in September and I have appreciated the darkness. It makes a longer time before I have to get up and face me and the world, [Mom wrote to Grandmom in 1969, in one of the two letters that survived the fire]. Sometimes I like the darkness too much. The dawn is great if one has the courage to go through one more day.
>
> Thurs. nite Frank and I saw Mr. B. (Mom's therapist in Margate) and I was very sullen. Wouldn't take off my sunglasses. I was hiding. Frank talked—my God, how he talked—maybe all we needed was an interpreter. Frank said to Mr. B. how I had asked him to someday bring me home a rose. I hadn't thought of that request in years. But Frank brought it up and there and then the whole discussion took off.
>
> Last night I remade my marriage vows and made a covenant with God. I finally went the last mile and gave in to everything. It won't be easy, I know, but the price is "absorbable." I feel truly good and clean for the first time in many a good long year.
>
> Thank you for coming when you did. I wanted my Mom. It would have been great if I could have done that 3 years ago, but look how much better it is now. Someone once said that God may close the door, but he leaves a window open.
>
> Mom, I love you. And my children and most of all, Frank. That's the way it should be. Finally.
>
> Love,
> Nancy

When I thought about my mother making her covenant with God and promises to Dad, paying her "absorbable" price, it became clear that her ambitions were high—too high. In this box of letters and old family papers, I had also found our school report cards, and the attendance records told their own story. Up until fourth grade or so, my absences seemed pretty normal. I wasn't winning any awards, but I showed up regularly.

After Mom returned home from her year in the hospital, though, I missed fourteen days of school that year. The next year was worse. And it was the same for my sisters. We all took turns staying home with Mom when she had bad nights and needed help. Looking into that box of papers, what opened up before me was a memory of the best hiding place ever.

I was proud of that hiding place. It was a really good one. Usually, I just stuck the bottles in a different cabinet or a bedroom closet or maybe in the front hall closet behind the coats. But that morning after my sisters left for school, my gaze fell on the cabinet door for the built-in ironing board near the utility room. I remembered the little cubbyhole below, where you might store an iron or a can of spray starch. Mom would never look there.

Mom had been bouncing in and out of hospitals for nearly two years at this point, and we had a routine: When Mom was home and Dad suspected she was on or headed for a bender, he would ask one of us girls to stay home and keep her out of the booze—except Liz. She was in kindergarten, for heaven's sake. He couldn't ask her. But Lisa, Leslie, and I all missed plenty of school, keeping an eye on Mom.

It was late spring in Brigantine, a school day morning, and Dad asked me to stay with Mom. She didn't have a good night, he said. "I need you to keep an eye on her." He told me to remember to hide the bottles, and then he left. I still remembered how nicely the bottles of gin and vermouth fit in the alcove below the built-in ironing board.

A couple of hours after breakfast, I was standing at the sink belatedly cleaning up dishes when Mom came down the stairs in the red velour bathrobe she wore all the time. I felt her annoyance to find me there, but she didn't say anything; she just started rummaging through the cabinets, moving stuff around, and feeling around behind the haphazardly stacked pots and pans and Pyrex casserole dishes. Becoming more desperate, she moved to the front hall closet. I could hear the hangers bang back and forth on the wooden pole as she continued her frantic search. I dried my hands on a nearby dishtowel, and she was back in the kitchen, staring directly at me now.

"Where is it?" Her voice was as flat and dark as a desert at night.

"Where is what?" This was a familiar game. I knew my role.

"You know what I'm talking about."

"No, I don't. Where is what?"

Mom took a quick step in my direction, screaming now, "Give me the goddamn booze. Give me the goddamn bottle."

I said, "No," but stepped backward and started to cry, feeling weak and afraid.

"I know Dad hid it and you know where. Show me where."

"I don't know what you're talking about," I yelled, but I was crying hard by then, so I didn't know what I really said. Then she was coming at me fast. You never wanted Mom to catch you when she was angry—never.

"Show me now," she growled.

Sobbing, I ducked her raised hand and scrambled around her, careful not to turn my back, and yanked open the ironing board cabinet.

Her eyes dropped down when she saw the bottles, and her face went blank. Emotionless, she stepped forward and retrieved the bottles while I dried my tears on the back of my hand. She rushed past me toward the stairs. I watched her go. When she was halfway up, though, some bright rage seized me, and I yelled at her, "You have to make a choice, Mom. It's us kids or the booze."

She turned halfway up the stairs, her face cracking into something like a smile, but it was nasty and hateful. "Oh, that's easy," she answered as she wagged the bottles she was grasping by the necks. "You see my choice." I heard her bedroom door slam, and I didn't think I saw her again that day.

I didn't know why I yelled that at Mom. It's not like I had any authority or could change her mind. But I had let Dad down. I was supposed to keep an eye on Mom and not let her find the booze. I failed miserably, and there would be hell to pay tonight when Dad found out.

The next day, I was allowed to go back to school. My fourth grade teacher asked each of us in the classroom to describe a family activity—something we all did together. One after another, my classmates stood up next to their desks and recited something or another. Boys and girls described going out to dinner at the local sub shop or attending Little League Baseball games or spending the day at the beach. I could hardly hear them for the roaring in my ears. When it was my turn, I dutifully stood and with calm conviction said, "I hate my mother."

Mrs. Simon tried to get me to take it back, but I just stood there stubborn and mute. So she gave me a special assignment: Engage in a family activity like a game or a puzzle that night and report back the next day. I was a good and obedient student, but I felt a flash of hatred for Mrs. Simon right then too.

When I got home from school, the house was quiet. Mom was sleeping upstairs, and the breakfast dishes were still piled high in the sink, soaking in cold water with a grayish film of detergent floating on top. I started to clean up the dishes and wipe down the counters still covered in crumbs from breakfast and the makings of sandwiches for lunch. As my sisters drifted in, we divided up the rest of the house chores and started our homework. Dad came home around 4:30 p.m., and we talked about what to eat for supper.

Mom made an appearance at the supper table, ate a few bites, said little or nothing, and went back upstairs to her bedroom. We never played a game that night, and the next day, I was too ashamed to tell Mrs. Simon the truth. I always did my homework. When she finally called on me, I thought about the Rogges' cabinet filled with board games and blurted out the first thing that came to memory. I told her we played chess. It was a ridiculous lie, and I didn't know the first thing about chess, but she seemed satisfied and turned her attention away.

Even now, I remembered the incident at school as a terrifying slipup, a direct violation of the Overton code. The Overton code was clear: We were to get straight As, keep our clothes clean and neatly ironed, and always be on our best behavior. Politeness was mandatory. Perfection was expected. We must not lie, bring attention to ourselves, and cause trouble or any extra worry—ever. And we never talked to anyone, even each other, about things that went on in our house.

It occurred to me now I might have been the only one who followed the code or knew about it at all. I remembered holding fast to the idea of being a perfect girl as a talisman against pain and chaos. The code protected me, I thought, and at least that gave me comfort.

More and more, I became Dad's helper. He relied on me when Mom was sick and confided in me when she had been up all night drinking or roaming the house or reading a book with the lights on. We called it insomnia. My sisters and I would talk about chores that needed to be done—the laundry, cleaning the bathrooms, and cooking—and I would take charge and divide up the work.

We had terrible fights about those chores. My sisters yelled that I wasn't their mother and I could not tell them what to do. But I was the one in charge, I hollered back, because Mom was sick. Then we all started screaming and hitting each other, usually three against one. At times, I would break down and cry. It wasn't fair that I was the oldest. Why wouldn't they help me? Everything was my responsibility.

I tried to make it fun and make a game out of cleaning house on Saturday mornings. We grabbed buckets, mops, rags, Ajax cleanser, and Pledge furniture polish and started cleaning the house, playing record albums loudly, and singing along. Leslie usually chose the music. We cleaned to the sounds of Herb Alpert and the Tijuana Brass and the 5th Dimension and their song "Up, Up and Away." These records were Mom's favorites. On a good day, it felt like she was there with us. In a few hours, the house was spotless, and we could escape to play with our friends.

Well-intentioned but nosy Mrs. Tagmeyer, who loved kids, lived across the street. She had no children of her own, so she had no one to whom she could pass along her hard-won knowledge of how to keep white clothes white or tenderize tough beef by adding a little white vinegar. But we could always count on her. Every so often, she came to our front door, asking what I was making for dinner and offering to help out or teaching me how to properly hang clothes on the line. Life was definitely more peaceful when Mom was gone.

During those years of wild promises and incessant relapse, Mom did make an effort. She took the barbiturates as prescribed—not realizing that they would make her depression worse—and sometimes she managed to drag herself out of bed long enough to be a mom. When my face broke out in my first preteen pimples, she took me to the pharmacy and helped me select the special face washes and creams that would quickly clear up my skin. She made certain I had Kotex pads and knew how to use them months before I started my period. I remembered this incident largely for the very graphic discussion about where babies came from, which still sounded pretty gross to me. During another one of our little mother-daughter chats, Mom explained to me that if one were serious about committing suicide, she would cut down her arm from the wrist, following the major veins. If one were simply seeking attention, she would cut side to side, just under the heel of her hand. I didn't want this information, not at all. I shut down and walked away.

What was the source of that darkness that rose so early? In a story Mom wrote about her life that I found among her papers—a story that seemed to be a kind of therapy or an attempted audit of her psyche—she said her "willfulness" began early:

> The kingdom was very poor when the little princess (that's Mom) was born and the Queen had to work very hard as well as the King, for they wanted to give the little princess everything she desired. But the little princess was a very unhappy and willful child. She always wanted everything her way and would cry and kick and scream if she didn't get it. Even when the Queen Mother gave her another little princess to play with, it only enraged the little princess. Now the little princess, being a sullen and bad behaved

child, never seemed to get anything she wanted, while her sister, who was a sunny and happy child (that's Aunt Jill she's talking about) always seemed to have everything go her way.

Finally, one day the little princess found she had grown to be quite a beautiful princess and thought that there was more than one way to skin a cat (as her grandmother would say). She would be nice to the Old King and Queen Mother and everyone else and then she would get all the things she wanted. Well, this was a very good idea, but the beautiful princess was nice for the wrong reasons and even when people admired her and she got most of the things she wanted, she was still unhappy.

She decided then to marry and show the entire world how to raise beautiful and good and wonderful princes and princesses for she thought, only I really know how because if I remember how unhappy I was as a child then I shall know how to make my children happy. Well, sure enough a prince came along and they were married. But, the beautiful princess married a prince very much like the Old King and he too let the beautiful princess have her own way and do everything she wanted.

Does everyone feel tempted to diagnose a troublesome parent after death? I did not accept the fact that Mom was mentally ill until late in my adulthood. I found myself thumbing through psychiatric descriptions and definitions, trying to understand the mercurial woman of my childhood. I was hoping that a psychiatric label would make her knowable or smaller or forgivable.

A few lines from Lewis Carroll's *Alice's Adventures in Wonderland* describe our situation.

"But I don't want to go among mad people," Alice remarked.

"Oh, you can't help that," said the Cat: "we're all mad here. I'm mad. You're mad."

"How do you know I'm mad?" said Alice.

"You must be," said the Cat, "or you wouldn't have come here."

Mom certainly showed signs of a mood disorder at a very young age and was eventually diagnosed with manic depression. She was more complicated than that. There was a strong vein of narcissism too. Her grandiosity, need for admiration, and lack of empathy were on full display long before she met Dad. She pegged Dad for an enabler just like her dad, the sweet old king. She wrote that this was unfortunate, but I thought an enabler was exactly what Mom was looking for.

What Mom did not capture in this self-critical fairy tale was her charm. She had flashing eyes and a quick smile. She was smart and funny and loved to flirt. In high school, according to Grandmom, Nancy developed early, became nervous, and ended up with ulcers. With stomach ulcers and the braces on her teeth, she went to high school every day that first year with a lunch of cream cheese and sardines. In spite of this, she became a popular girl and soaked up enough confidence to go away to the University of Connecticut.

According to letters between Mom and Grandmom, Mom suffered horrible bouts of homesickness in those two years she attended UConn. Nancy was elected to the court of the Football Hop Queen, but was so unhappy that she eventually came home for good. According to Aunt Jill and Mom's friend Millie, Mom was actually forced to leave the university after she was caught in bed with another girl. Mom told Jill that they were just comforting each other through their homesickness, but nobody really believed her. That was Nancy—high and low, wild and meek.

In her fairy tale, Mom described these early years as bliss. Dad lost a job when his company moved away, but Grandmom and Grandpa stepped in to pay Dad's tuition to attend Seton Hall and earn a teaching credential. Dad worked part-time as a janitor cleaning the men's urinals at the Plumbers Union Hall next door to Grandmom's house. Money was always tight.

> Then after ten years had passed the Prince decided to take the beautiful princess and all the beautiful little grand princesses and move to another kingdom. Now this might have been very good, but once again there was never enough money and the beautiful Princess needed the Old Queen and her family and friends very much. For in the old Kingdom she was somebody and in this new Kingdom she was nobody. And she became unhappier and unhappier.
>
> She drank too much wine all the time and kept nagging the prince to make things better. Pretty soon the beautiful princess could stand it no longer. She took a lot of pills and tried to die. But the little princesses and the prince found her in time and took her to a place to get well.

In the moments when she was able, Mom would draw us into craft projects or try to make a meal into a party. Or she would shake off the pharmaceutical fog and try to recreate the *IT girl* she imagined herself to be.

Once, it was with a paper dress. It was 1968, and Mom was fascinated with the youth movement. She liked the way women could be attractive and seem independent by wearing kicky little dresses. A revolution was happening for modern women, and Mom wanted to be part of it, so she bought herself a paper dress.

That dress was the latest thing in fashion, she assured us girls. It was a sleeveless A-line dress with a crew collar, printed with a simple-yet-loud graphic pattern. If a child cut a paper dress out of a colorful magazine page, it would look very similar.

"Look at this dress. It is fantastic," she told us on Saturday, twirling it through the air so it snapped and spun over our heads.

"Nobody in this town will have anything like it. I'll wear it to church tomorrow, and when I'm done, I will use it to mop the floor!"

Mom frosted her hair and trimmed up her pixie cut. It was like she was getting ready for a date, although Mom and Dad never went to movies or restaurants because money was always tight. Church was the only "out" to go to. The next morning, Dad was not happy. Mom was determined to actually go to church wearing the paper dress with the suntan-colored pantyhose that came out of a white plastic egg. He said it was inappropriate, and they both fumed until it was time to leave. Dad couldn't be late because he sang tenor in the choir.

Secretly, I thought Mom looked pretty with her frosted hair, pink lipstick, and short, colorful dress showing off her tanned legs. I would not side against Dad, though. Steadily through the service and the coffee hour afterward, Mom grew more brittle. Dad ignored her entirely. Nobody gushed over her dress or her fun and modern sensibilities, no matter how many times she twirled and encouraged people to touch the material. It was a paper towel!

During the car ride home from the church, we could feel Mom's anger mounting. When we arrived at the house, she stomped into the living room, grabbed the front of the dress in both her fists, and yanked and tugged until it ripped jaggedly down the back and came off in one horrible whoosh. She threw it down at her feet and stood there a moment, breathing hard in her white bra, suntan pantyhose and medium heels. Another woman might have cried, but Mom whipped her head around to face the stairs and marched up to change. The rest of us quickly grabbed swimsuits and escaped to our white-sand beach where nothing was so bad it couldn't be swept out to sea.

In 1972, our final year in Brigantine, the gas heat was shut off for nonpayment in the middle of a frigid January. Our only car, Dad's new Oldsmobile station wagon that he loved to drive, was repossessed. Mom's mood swings were increasing in frequency and velocity. One day, she would be earnestly discussing sex with me, telling me it was a beautiful thing and I would be on birth control soon enough. The next, she would be sitting down in the spare bedroom, staring at the wall all day with a blanket covering her head. Other times, she bounced back up and decided to take the dog for a walk.

During the Brigantine years, we had a pedigreed English bull-dog named Winston Oglethorpe Overton, or Winnie. He was a gift for my Dad, who needed a "son," Mom said. Winnie was so ugly he was cute, and we all loved him. He was one of those dogs that would curl up in a warm spot and nap until summoned for a walk. It was mostly Dad who walked Winnie. Sometimes, one of us girls walked Winnie down to one of the nearby vacant lots so he could relieve himself. Mom mostly ignored the dog, unless he was snoring too loudly or farting.

This particular afternoon following a long dark period, Mom was suddenly up and energetic again. When we arrived home from school, she was showered and had lipstick on, but the house was not clean. Nor did it smell like dinner was cooking. We settled uneasily around the kitchen table to do homework, listening to Mom move around upstairs.

And then she was in the kitchen, wearing her blue denim skirt, knee socks and penny loafers, and a cable-knit sweater. Pulling on her favorite jean jacket, she announced she was going to take Winnie for a walk. Mom's face was a plastic mask. We looked at her.

"I'm going to take Winnie for a walk," she repeated, "and when I get home, I'm going to kill him."

Liz cried first, and Lisa said, "No!" I stood up from the table as Mom turned with her scary not-human mask still on and called for Winnie to come to her.

It was Lisa who scrambled and caught Winnie. Lisa grabbed him by the collar, ducked, and ran with him into the downstairs bathroom. She slammed the door. I was rocking forward and back-ward in place, trying to figure out how to get in Mom's way without getting hurt, when Mom banged open the door to the utility room, disappeared, and then emerged with a sledge hammer swinging from her right hand. It was big and heavy, well scarred from use. Mom swung the hammer forward a little and let it propel her toward the bathroom door while we shrunk from her path.

"Mom, no!" In my memory, I was still in that hall with her. I was two feet away, my hand reaching for the hammer, impossibly brave. And I was simultaneously ten feet away wearing cast-iron shoes, cringing in fear.

I was yelling and yelling, but she never heard me as she slammed the hammer again into the bathroom door screaming, "Now, I'm going to kill both of you." Later, people tried to explain. They said Mom was ill and did not know what she was doing. But she used my sister's name. She said, "Lisa, open this door, or I will kill you too. I will kill you, Lisa, like I'm going to kill the dog."

Somebody ran to a neighbor's house for help. It must have been Liz or Leslie because I thought I was rooted to the floor, helpless and waiting for a chance to intervene.

The neighbor called Dad, who was at Thursday night choir practice. He raced home, and after he put Mom to bed, everyone calmed down. Lisa and Winnie left the bathroom safely. Mom disappeared again, whether into herself or into a hospital. I didn't remember. Somehow we all went on, hurtling toward the inevitable.

1972–1974

BURK COURT

Those who hate most fervently must
have once loved deeply; those who
want to deny the world must have once
embraced what they now set on fire.
——Stephen King

Family dinner with the neighbors, circa 1972

How could I arrive at the root of my sister's culpability? I loved Jill and Doug, but was not satisfied with their conclusions. They had no confession, no gasoline-soaked rags. Still, when I thought about going with Lisa to Brigantine that summer of 2012 to dig up the past, I could not shake the vague feeling of unease, of threat. I went back to the pages of the reports.

On July 11, 1974, Lt. Thomas Dougherty wrote the memo saying that Buzby and Fields were "going to blow the case wide open" with some interviews. Two days later, Fields and Rutley reinterviewed Lisa and her best friend, Beth. Both girls told the exact same story they told before. But that very same day, the investigators received two new pieces of information: A teenage girl—or her mother— reported that one of us said, "They're dead. We're free now." And Dennis Kelly, principal of Ventnor Middle School, called to report that Lisa approached another student, Joey C., a week before the fire and asked him how to start one.

When I got Dennis Kelly on the phone more than forty years after the fact, he repeated to me exactly what he told the police. He still believed there was something to the allegation.

"Lisa was very bright and very troubled," Dennis Kelly told me. "It was not a good combination. I remember that she came into my office once, quite upset, and she kept saying 'I didn't do it.' But I don't know what she was referring to. Kids were talking about the rumors of how Lisa started the fire or wanted someone to start a fire, but I never heard that from an adult," he said.

I asked if he thought Lisa could have started the fire, even accidentally, and then completely block out the memory or maybe the fire could have been connected to her drug dealing.

"That's possible," he said. "Lisa was involved in the drug scene, and it could have been someone from her group. I have to tell you theirs was the craziest class of kids we ever had. Any one of the teachers from that time would confirm it."

After saying goodbye to Principal Kelly, I spent a while staring at the telephone. He remembered Lisa coming in to his office saying, "I didn't do it." He was very clear about this. Yet, the fire occurred a week after Lisa graduated from eighth grade and left that school. She could not have been referring to the fire. Come to think of it. I was not even sure how the principal could have been hearing all these rumors from kids when the fire was set during summer break.

Yet, there was no denying that he absolutely believed what he was saying. He had reason to think Lisa was responsible.

One thing I had learned over these years while returning to this file again and again was that, in the absence of official answers, the truth became the shifting view from inside a kaleidoscope. One report or another would float to the surface and dominate my view, sending a new set of facts clicking into place, casting doubt on one person and then another. The roles of victim and arsonist were recast with such frequency that I easily lost my footing.

Just then I was staring again at a Ventnor PD property report and thinking, *Where the hell did Dad get $2,500?*

There was a strong box found near my mother's body in the master bedroom, according to this report; and inside were various items of jewelry, a gold watch, and cash and checks equaling $2,561. My dad made $8,800 a year. When he got a raise to that amount, he proudly posted the letter on the refrigerator. Adjusted for the average salary of an Atlantic City schoolteacher in 2012, that $2,500 was like finding nearly $18,000 in the ashes of a suspicious fire that took out a hard-luck family.

Where did Dad get the money? I knew he was not working during the summer of 1974. He was hanging around the house refinishing furniture and seemed to have no prospects of a summer job. They were, as always, deeply in debt. And yet here was a small fortune in cash and checks, noted in fourteen separate line item entries ranging from $202.35 to $53.93. Each entry, however, was only an amount, a number. There was no indication of where the checks came from.

The strong box was delivered to our lawyer, Maurie Cole. The jewelry was eventually divided between us girls. The money, I was told, was lumped in with the rest of the estate. What I wanted to know was where that money came from and what it might have had to do with the fire. When I called the Coles, however, Maurie's wife, Linda, told me that Maurie was doing poorly. He'd been in a nursing facility for a few years and only occasionally recognized her. All his records had been destroyed. I persisted and even tracked down

Maurie's former legal secretary, but the answers were always the same, "I'm sorry. I can't help you."

Was I crazy for thinking about loan sharks? I knew Dad tried to get conventional bank loans and was turned down. There were no high-interest credit cards with cash advances or easy mortgages in those days, but there were neighborhood guys who could help out. They didn't break your knees unless you stopped paying. Had Dad found a temporary fix for our finances, fallen behind, and brought retribution on our heads? This was not as melodramatic as it sounded. This was, after all, pre-casino Atlantic City. It was a grittier place, full of secrets and stinking of desperation. The Vietnam War was grinding on with no end in sight; we were in the middle of a recession, an oil crisis, and runaway inflation. In New Jersey of 1974, there were 403.4 violent crimes per 100,000 people. (By 2011, that number had dropped to 308.4.) People seemed inured to a certain level of violence so long as it stayed on the cheaper side of town. And there we were in the shoddy Waterview townhomes, every window open on a hot night, two sets of sliding glass doors thrown open and waiting. A paid arsonist could have easily slipped inside and made an example of us.

Dad was always looking for money. He wasn't working that summer. Where did he get the money to finance that break? Of course, taking out a neighborhood loan would have been risky, but Dad was at the end of his rope. He told me as much, shortly before the fire.

Dad's fights with Mom, when she was lucid, grew more volatile overtime. One night, I heard them shouting at each other in the den. I knew they were in their usual positions: Mom in her red velour robe on the blue-plaid couch and Dad in the skirted chair, peering at the television set from behind his thick glasses with the heavy black frames. Alongside the television set sat a low bookcase Dad built using walnut-stained pine shelves stacked on red bricks.

On this particular night, I stood in my bedroom doorway, listening because this fight was higher pitched than usual. I needed to know what was coming. I heard a strange strangled scream, then a crash, a grunt, and stunned silence. I crept downstairs, fast and quiet, and then snuck my head around the den's doorjamb. The top shelf of the bookcase was askew. Mom was standing there with her arms folded across her chest, her face closed in shock. Dad cradled his black glasses in his hand like a broken bird; his other hand was pressed against the side of his head, blood oozing through his fingers and dripping down his neck onto his shirt.

"Nance," he said in a quaking voice, outraged but losing steam. "Goddamnit, Nance, you broke my glasses." His voice shuddered again, and he started to cry. A red brick from the bookcase had dented the paneling behind Dad's chair. A dusty red scrape on the wall outlined the flight path of the brick on its way to the carpet after hitting Dad in the face. "Goddamnit," Dad sobbed. Mom sat down heavily on the couch and leaned forward, her head rocking back and forth. "I'm bleeding. I need to go to the hospital, Nance," he said thickly. "My glasses."

Dad was nearly blind without his glasses. I knew he didn't have money to replace them. I could not believe Mom would be so stupid. I backed away from the doorway, retreated to my room, and softly shut the door.

As teenagers, Lisa and Leslie were in open rebellion, ignoring any rules Dad tried to set. In his battles with his daughters and his wife, he continued to lose ground. "Don't smoke" became "Don't let me see you smoke" and later "Don't smoke in your bedroom." Still, the house was saturated in a nicotine fug. One day, Detective Fields rang the doorbell and told Dad that Lisa was stealing Mom's pills and selling them to her middle school friends. Who wouldn't be desperate?

I thought back to one of the last conversations I had with Dad.

On Wednesday night, the week of the fire, he had been waiting up for me. Dad always stayed up until the last sister was home. Dad was alone in the den, sitting in his easy chair in the corner. He gestured to the couch when I put my head in the room to say goodnight.

"Your grades were good again this year," he said. "I am very proud of you."

"Thanks," I said. I had just finished my junior year in high school. Praise was infrequent in our house.

"You'll be thinking about where to go to college next year," he said. "Have you thought about what you'll study?"

"I like psychology," I said carefully. He still seemed to be listening, so I ventured further. "Actually, if I can get my math scores up, I'd like to be a psychiatrist, I think."

"A doctor?"

"Yes. Someone who could help, you know, people like Mom."

Dad nodded slowly. Nobody ever talked to me about college. It was my secret dream, to go away to college like Mom had, to sleep in a dorm and start a life away from the family. I did not know if he would take me seriously or even support the idea.

"Well, you're a smart girl. You could go to a lot of different schools. I hope you'll go far away."

"Away?"

"Yes, as far away from here as you can get."

We both sat for a moment. It was hot and stuffy in that room, even with the sliding doors opened wide. I just wanted to get ready for bed.

"I'm sorry," he said. "It's been so rough around here." He shook his head slowly and pushed his heavy glasses back up on his nose. "I don't know what to do. I may have to give up custody on your sisters. Lisa and Les may end up going to the state. I don't know how to control them anymore, and they are making things hard for your mom. I need to look after her too." I nodded and made a sympathetic noise. Dad continued on talking as if to himself. "If your sisters don't start behaving and staying out of trouble, I just can't have it," he said. "I just can't have it."

"I know," I whispered. "I know."

I felt sorry for him, but I had to get up and go to work in the morning. I said good night and went upstairs. I couldn't fall asleep. Why would Dad tell me he was going to give up my sisters? I knew they acted badly, but sending them away was extreme. Besides, Mom was a big part of the problem. What was Dad going to do about Mom? I thought about what he said about going as far away from home as possible. That made sense to me. I just wasn't sure how I was going to do it.

It sounded barbaric now, in this age where people fought long court battles to keep custodial rights of their children. But in the 1970s, parents still threatened children with the orphanage or reform school or simply "the state" when they broke the rules. This was the year Linda Blair showed us exactly what juvenile detention meant in her made-for-television movie *Born Innocent.* Lisa and Leslie would be branded as juvenile delinquents, be forced to wear scratchy uniforms, fistfight other girls, and go to bed every night knowing that nobody loved them. As far as I was concerned at the time, they deserved it.

Dad also told me that Mom's doctors were threatening to keep her in a mental hospital for good if she attempted suicide again. They told Dad there was a state law about it or something. So Dad, deeply in debt, was on the precipice of losing his wife and giving up two daughters. Maybe he snapped and set the fire on impulse without really thinking about us. Maybe he just wanted the train of failures to stop. When I added up the strikes against him, arson became a perverse, logical answer.

Curiously, I didn't feel particularly angry with Dad when I thought about the possibility of him setting the fire. Maybe it's more correct to say that the mixture of anger and pity and sorrow I usually felt in regard to my dad was largely unchanged. I tried to justify the choices he was contemplating; but it became more like a stone in my shoe, ever-present and annoying, but not crippling.

But what about Mom?

A dozen empty prescription bottles found by firefighters in my mother's dresser drawer and a flood of memories led me into the dark forest of Mom's psychiatric condition. We did not talk much about it at the time and certainly did not use the term mental illness. We called it bad behavior or Mom just being Mom. We did not understand that she was in the grip of an illness. Even as an adult, I thought of Mom as willful and impulsive, aggravating, and untrustworthy, rather than mentally ill. It was easier to be angry.

After piecing together a few clues and using the list of drugs from the fire investigators' report, I concluded it was Mom who should have been angry. Bounced from hospital to home like a rubber ball with no continuity of care, Mom's treatment consisted largely of prescriptions for highly addictive medications. By this time, she was no longer responsible for her choices, and the expert advice she paid for did its own damage.

In the eight years between her first suicide attempt and her death, Mom rotated in and out of mental hospitals at least a dozen times. Dad explained to us kids that she was going in to "dry out" after a serious drinking binge or a suicide attempt and escalating bad behavior got her committed. In between hospitalizations, she was sent home with a bottle or two of pills and a pep talk about fulfilling her duties as wife and mother. She didn't have anyone to talk to once she was discharged. We did not have health insurance that covered psychiatric visits—a rare benefit in those days—so she came home and sometimes talked to us.

She told us what various doctors said and, sometimes, specifics about her therapy. Once, Mom told me that her therapist was trying to help with Mom's anxiety over the condition of my sisters' bedroom. The girls refused to keep the room clean; and Mom had utterly failed, she thought, to change my sisters' behavior. Mom's therapist tried teaching her acceptance. He told Mom to live in her room at the hospital for an entire week without picking anything up. Where things landed, they stayed. Mom hated living like her daughters, but the experience gave her a coping skill. When she returned home, she could look in at my sisters' room and then shut the door. If she could not see the mess, it did not exist.

In the year following her first suicide attempt, Mom was given the new mood-stabilizing wonder drug, Lithium. She boasted to us that it was experimental and she was a pioneer guinea pig. She loved the attention. She also liked Librium, Valium, and the uppers she took when she was trying to stay awake during the day so she could sleep at night. Mom got comfortable with drugs. Once I was in the kitchen when she came downstairs, retrieved a tiny ampule from the refrigerator, and hiked up her skirt. Aghast, I watched as she jammed a syringe into the bottle and then jabbed it into her thigh. She looked up suddenly from under that dark fringe of hair cut short like Mia

Farrow's and saw me standing there. This time, her eyes softened, and she explained that it was vitamin B12 for energy.

Mom liked to experiment. She kept a bottle of belladonna on a small shelf above the kitchen sink where none of us could reach it. She and Dad had a horrible fight about it one day. It was during a brief dry spell at our house. Dad accused Mom of being intoxicated. Mom protested loudly, yelling at Dad that she was not intoxicated; the belladonna was making her act that way. She claimed it was therapy, but according to what I read about belladonna, it was usually taken recreationally for the vivid hallucinations and delirium it could provoke. I supposed this explained why Dad was so angry and why Mom liked it so much.

There were people who had heard my story and quickly pointed to Mom as the likely culprit. A narcissistic, bipolar alcoholic suffering from profound depression—wouldn't she be your first suspect? Maybe this was just her biggest suicide attempt yet. But I could not believe her capable of anything so premeditated. I tried to imagine her methodically sloshing a flammable liquid—even a bottle of vodka—up the stairs, over the threshold of her bedroom doorway, into my bedroom, and down the hall (but not into Lisa's room) and then lighting a match; but I was stopped cold on two fronts. One, she would never waste vodka like that. Two, she was too strung out on various medications to execute anything so deliberate.

My sisters? Leslie, at sixteen, did not have a mean bone in her body and was a little too much of a follower in her younger days to have set a fire. Liz was only twelve, and I was sure she was sound asleep before I woke her up. Neither one had ever shown signs of aggression.

I always came back around to Lisa. I could see her running around the corner of the town house that fire-lit night, bright eyed, with that wristwatch glinting on her arm. Angry all the time and indifferent to consequences, Lisa was absolutely smart enough to lay a trail of flammable liquid, running it into my bedroom but not hers, light a match downstairs, run back up to her bed, and wait.

I supposed there was someone in every family on whom suspicion fell first. If you told any gathered family that there was a missing pearl necklace, a questionable fire, a police investigation, all heads would swivel in the same direction. Lisa was our *usual suspect*. It wasn't a random selection; she had earned that place by sneaking out windows, smoking pot, and being in constant and open defiance of authority. Then again, she was only fourteen.

1973

CROSS-COUNTRY CAMPING TRIP

Sometimes you never know the true value
of a moment until it becomes a memory.
—Dr. Seuss

Leigh, Liz, Leslie, and Lisa in San Francisco, 1973

It wasn't until 1973, while camping at Refugio Beach State Park in California, that I learned what was behind my father's decision to take our family across country during that summer. Gathered at a campground potluck, the adult conversation spilled into the kids' circles.

"I always regretted that decision," I overhead him say to another camper, a woman named Lois. She and her husband, Jim, had established a quick relationship with my parents; and a campfire bond developed. My father had been telling Lois that after he was discharged from the Army in Hawaii in 1946, he returned home to New Jersey by plane. He was only nineteen, after all, and his youthful desire to put his feet back on native soil overrode any penchant for adventure. But several of his Army buddies took the long way home, cruising across the Pacific by ship and ambling across the country by slow train. Their tales of purple mountains' majesties and descriptions of the beauty and expanse of our country kindled in my father a new line item on his bucket list: nationwide road trip.

Until 1972, the national teachers association had always convened in Atlantic City, and my father was an annual delegate.

"But last year," he confided in Lois, "a woman was passing out flyers, telling us to come to her city for this year's convention. I asked her where, and she told me, 'Portland, Oregon.' I promised her I'd be there."

He traded in the family station wagon for a newer model; procured somehow a brand-new, twenty-one-foot, two-axle Coachman trailer; and sublet our town house. He packed up Mom, my sisters and me, and our family dog, Winnie, as well as Genie-girl, Mom's Siamese cat; and we headed out to the open road.

Our family was no stranger to camping, but this upgrade to a recreational vehicle from the typical Sears and Roebuck tent we were used to made us feel like we were pulling a palace behind our car. The plan was to head west to Portland, stopping in state and national parks along the way. The whole summer and the open road stretched out before us. Dad's cousins in Southern California peopled the itinerary, and Mom wanted to see Death Valley and other national parks. She seemed to be in a holding pattern as far as her mental health went. I supposed the rigors of life on the road helped keep her thinking focused on the tasks of daily living. Maybe waking up in one location and going to sleep several hundred miles away was like a geographical lobotomy: The constantly changing surroundings literally put the past behind you, because there is nothing in your present to remind you of what went on back there.

My boyfriend Allan, whom I left in New Jersey with promises to send postcards along our route, had taken a summer job with Allied Van Lines. I recruited my sisters to help as spotters for the big orange tractor-trailer with the black triangle and white interstate marker emblazoned on the side. Every orange truck we spotted marked a lifeline to my faraway lover.

Our routine settled in easily, driving during daylight hours with stops for meals and rest breaks and then finding a campground for the evening. We packed up the trailer the next morning after breakfast and then piled back into the car to continue the westbound journey. Our first stop was Dayton, Ohio, where Mom's Aunt Arlene and Uncle Hyman lived in plastic slipcover splendor. Aunt Arlene's blue-tinted hair rose above her head high enough to make us wonder what held it up there. A fluffy white designer dog accompanied us as we swam in their built-in swimming pool in the backyard of their fancy sprawling rancher.

Snippets of the trip memories from each of us sisters are all the more poignant because this was to be our final family trip before the fire. Liz and Lisa remember buying soda in a store near Davenport, Iowa.

"Two bottles of pop," twanged the yokel behind the cash register.

"Of *what?*" the girls wanted to know.

"Pop, you know, soda pop. Yawl want that in a sack?"

"A *what?*" They stared at him blankly until he waved a paper bag at them.

"A sack!"

Who knew we'd have to learn a new language for the trip?

A little campground nestled in Cheyenne, Wyoming, afforded us shelter for one night. After swimming in the pool, we walked into town and bought fireworks. Anyone from the East Coast knows fireworks are illegal to purchase at home, but there in Wyoming, even kids could buy them cheaply in 1973.

Another relaxed law in Wyoming allowed my parents to wake up early, pack up the trailer, and continue our journey westward while Les, Liz, and I remained sleeping in the trailer. Early-riser Lisa lounged across the back seat of the car, an act not possible when six of us rode together. Constant motion kept us trailer riders lulled into an extra hour and a half of shut-eye. When my sisters and I woke up, we signaled through the windows to Lisa, who informed Dad we were awake. A rest area on I-80 across from Elk Mountain provided a place to pull off the highway so we could prepare breakfast.

But everyone lost their appetite when we realized Genie-girl wasn't among the sleeping beauties. After a hasty family conference, it was decided Mom and I would head back to Cheyenne to locate our feline sister. Dad unhooked the trailer, and we headed east. An uneventful hour-and-a-half drive later, we pulled back in to the trailer campground. Mom got out of the car and called for her Genie-girl. Almost immediately we heard a responding cry. Using patience and echolocation, Mom calling out and Genie responding, we located our Genie-girl under the office trailer. Mom crawled under and pulled her out, Genie clinging to Mom. Another hour-and-a-half drive back west, Genie tightly curled up on Mom's lap. We reunited with the rest of our anxious family.

Lisa reported that their wait was not uneventful. First, the girls decided to walk across the interstate to the mountain right across the street. They crossed the highway, climbed through a barbed wire fence, and set out across a marshy field. After thirty minutes of slogging, their feet soaked, the mountain was no closer. Later, after examining a map, they learned the mountain was actually about seven miles away. They returned to the rest area, and Dad brought out his binoculars. Off in the distance, antelope played out on the range. Dad and Lisa were setting off firecrackers, mounting them on the barbs of the fence and lighting them. Watching the antelope through the binoculars, they could be seen jumping, startled, at each bang of the firecrackers. Maybe they thought they were under heavy fire, or it was just a dry run before the start of the hunting season.

Our dog, Winnie, lay sleeping in the shade under the back end of the trailer, trying to keep cool. Cars whizzed by on the interstate. One old wood-paneled station wagon abruptly screeched to a halt and backed up into the rest area. It turned out the occupants included a brindle bulldog named Babe. Someone in their car had spotted Winnie, and they stopped to chat and take photos of the dogs together—canine love on the interstate.

After a few hours passed without any sight of Mom and me, Dad began to feel anxious. Mom was known for her unpredictability. There was no way to contact her, no way to know if Mom and I had made it back to the campground or even if we were coming back. What the hell was he supposed to do if she didn't return? Three daughters, a bulldog, and a trailer without means to tow it. But before his anxiety morphed into full-blown panic, Mom and I careened into the rest stop, jubilant, with Genie-girl in her arms. Dad, relieved, quickly hooked the trailer back up; and we headed on down the highway. We only drove as far as Rawlins before we stopped for the night. From there, we made it to a KOA campground near Twin Falls, Idaho; and the next day, we arrived in Portland. While Dad was away at the convention, Mom took us girls sightseeing around Portland. Lisa remembered there was no sales tax when we bought some candy from a store. Leslie recalled a boat ride on the Willamette River, and each of us could still picture the beauty of the Portland Japanese Garden.

From Portland, we meandered south, spending one night at Beverly Beach on the Pacific Ocean, where we scoured the sand in search of agates. We headed inland and experienced Crater Lake. Dad filled the gas tank, and we headed back to the road, but gravel construction slowed our progress. Then Dad noticed the gas gauge needle leaning leftward at the same time someone yelled, "I smell gas!" We coasted into a dealership in Yreka, where it was discovered a sharp pebble had sliced through a rubber tube in the gas line. We lost a full tank of gas, in addition to the cost of repair, and Dad was not happy.

As Mom's bucket list shortened, Dad's money supply shrunk. We crossed the Golden Gate Bridge and rode the cable cars in San Francisco. A seafood restaurant on Fisherman's Wharf served prawns, where we consumed the only meal not cooked in our trailer kitchen, pretending to be rich tourists on holiday. We wanted to see Alcatraz, but the boat fare across the San Francisco bay for a family of six was not in the budget. So we found a place to legally park the car with the trailer and explored the city on foot. I fell in love with San Francisco and vowed that I would one day return.

Leaving my heart in San Francisco, we continued our journey. The Coast Highway twisted and turned us south. Dad, still not used to maneuvering a large trailer, struggled with the drive all the way to Morro Bay. Liz said she worked as the navigator and Mom sat in the back with Les, Lisa, and me. But I remembered taking control of the radio, endlessly fiddling with the dials. Dad's favorite song that year was "Diamond Girl," by Seals and Croft; and Mom preferred to sing along with Tony Orlando asking us to "Tie a Yellow Ribbon" around the old oak tree.

After a short stay at Morro Bay, we changed the venue to a beach where we could swim in the Pacific Ocean, at Refugio State Park. It was the first time I ever ate tacos, one evening when the neighbor campers invited us to share their meal. The next night, Mom reciprocated by cooking up a batch of her famous spaghetti and meatballs. Les and Liz got the worst sunburn, and Lisa contracted pink eye.

The Hollywood Freeway, CA 101, ferried us south to West Covina and Cousin Betty Lou. The fear Dad felt, driving on a six-lane freeway for the first time, kept us hushed in the back seats. Dad's New Jersey driving style was not suited to that kind of California traffic.

After a short visit with Betty Lou and her family, where she served us chicken teriyaki which none of us kids liked, we headed north again to Yosemite, with plans to hit Death Valley afterward. But campground scuttlebutt and words of wisdom from Betty Lou had warned us that Yosemite Valley was overrun with hippies, and no one would visit Death Valley in the summer. Mom and Dad pressed on anyway. After all, hippies were a peace-loving bunch of young people, and some of their ideology probably appealed to Mom's bohemian disposition—free love, high on nature, anti-war. If Mom had been younger, I bet she would've been marching with the protesters in faded ripped jeans, wearing a flower in long braided hair and a beaded, peace sign necklace.

As I mentioned, memories from this long-ago trip were not very well chronicled in any one of my sisters. Each of us, though, could clearly remember a picnic we had by the Merced River. Mom outdid herself grilling chicken with the family recipe barbecue sauce and serving macaroni salad with tuna and hard-boiled eggs to complement the pasta and celery. We dipped our feet into the icy-cold river and hiked up the Mist Trail, clambering over rocks, to the base of the Vernal Fall. The views took our breath away. Full of awe and gratitude, we were captivated by Mother Nature's splendor.

By this time, Dad realized his travel budget had been exceeded. We were flat-out broke. Arrangements were made that my grandmother would mail a check to us, General Delivery, Las Vegas. Our plan was to cross the Sierras into Nevada and head south to pick up the relief funds. Mom was still hoping to see Death Valley, but temperature readings above 105 degrees Fahrenheit left that line item on her bucket list unchecked.

In Las Vegas, Dad was pissed. The task of pulling all that weight over the mountains and into the southwestern desert caused the car engine to overheat, so using the air conditioner was not an option. Winnie, especially, suffered in the heat, his breath coming in deep, noisy, frightening gasps. After picking up the check, Dad visited several check-cashing places; and cursing up a storm about their usury practices, he instead found a bank where he could cash the check to continue our trip. Two hundred dollars, in 1973, barely supported us; but I supposed that's all Grandmom was willing to send. We headed south across the Hoover Dam into Arizona, hoping to see the Grand Canyon; but the combination of the car, the heat, and the dog's condition caused Dad to turn us around and head north.

By sundown, we located Overton Beach on the northern edge of Lake Mead. After taking photos, illuminated by the car's headlights, next to the sign, we headed north in the dark. Because of the daytime fiasco in Las Vegas, Dad refused to drive during the heat of day. We pulled into Zion National Park, where we camped. Bryce Canyon served as our surrogate for the missed Grand Canyon. Lisa remembered Dad showing Mom a moment of tenderness on a family hike. "We hiked down to the canyon floor, probably on the Navajo Loop Trail. Due to her heavy smoking, Mom was winded on the trek back up to the parking lot. Instead of his usual blame-the-victim stance, Dad stopped and waited until Mom caught her breath and was able to continue. He even publicly asked her if she was okay. I remember it because it was so unusual for him."

We packed up camp that evening and headed north again. Flaming Gorge Reservoir, tucked into the northeastern corner of Utah, served as our next stop. We probably camped at one of the free sites, spending the days swimming and the nights playing "Oh Hell!" card game. Genie-girl once again dictated what our plans were, because she left the trailer and didn't come back. Mom insisted we stay until Genie-girl returned. Mom and Dad argued about it, Dad probably worried about the severe shortage of travel funds while Mom was devoted to her precious cat.

One afternoon, all of us girls took our dog, Winnie, down to the reservoir to meet up with some boys we had met earlier and go for a swim. Splashing around in the water, laughing, and showing off, we didn't pay much attention to Winnie who swam out to us.

Winnie tried to get to us, anyway. His top-heavy build made him a lousy swimmer, and soon he was in trouble, gasping and flailing and nearly dogpaddling down to an early grave. One of the cute boys ran through the waist-deep water, churning his legs and throwing out his arms for balance, looking like a modern-day hero as he grabbed Winnie and dragged him to shore. With the help of another boy, they frantically massaged Winnie's stomach while the poor dog heaved up gallons of water, coughing and gagging. Then Winnie rolled over, staggered to his feet, shook himself off from the tip of his nose to his tail, and tried to get back into the water where Liz and Leslie were still swimming. Lisa grabbed Winnie, and we sisters walked him back to the campsite, swearing among ourselves that we would never tell Mom and Dad that we almost drowned the dog.

Finally, after five days waiting for the cat at Flaming Gorge, Dad laid down the law. We were leaving the next morning, with or without Genie. Our card playing that evening was less than enthusiastic. Mom was sulking, and I was sure she made Dad feel guilty about his decision.

Just as we were about to bid our hands, a distinct sound was heard at the trailer door.

"Meow!"

"Genie!" We all yelled at once. That one sound elevated us from the depths of family angst. The next morning, we continued north. Although Mom and Dad had mapped out our route before we left home, the vagaries of road travel and the strange habits of cats allowed for modifications.

I barely remembered Mount Rushmore. Lisa thought that's when Mom started drinking again. Leslie was sure something happened, but she didn't know what. But the family mood tightened after that. There were more arguments over what stations to play on the radio. We each took turns reading paperback novels, and by this time on the road trip, most of the good books had been read. No one cared about the big orange Allied moving vans, either. I stared anxiously out the window, now the only person who noticed my orange lifeline headed in the other direction. When we stopped to take a walk, I walked ahead of the others, not wanting to be part of my own family.

We wanted to see western Wyoming, where herds of bison roamed in the Grand Teton and Yellowstone; and Mom wanted to meet a real cowboy, but Dad nixed that trip, citing well-known cost overruns that thwarted many side activities. Instead, we camped at Blue Mounds State Park in Minnesota, where a herd of bison drew tourists because of their untainted DNA. Many of our nation's buffalo have interbred with cattle, and pure strains are rare indeed.

In Wisconsin, with money nearly gone, my mother sent us kids out to a neighboring cornfield to steal some corn on the cob for dinner. Her karma was evened out when the ears turned out to be inedible. A fellow camper told us that farmers planted tough horse corn on the outside rows, to thwart thieves like us from pirating their crops. We ate pancakes for dinner that night instead.

The rest of the trip home held no vibrant memories for any of us. Liz claimed Mom slept in the trailer, laws in the eastern United

States prohibiting such action be damned. I bet Dad didn't defy her only to keep peace in the family car. We couldn't return to our town house in Ventnor, because the subtenants were occupying our town-home until the middle of August. We headed to Fords instead, back to my grandmother's home.

As soon as we arrived, I called Allan, who arrived at Grandmom's two hours later. Grandmom was not very happy. A few months earlier, her hip was broken when she was attacked by an inmate at the prison where she worked for the last twenty-five years. She was sixty-two then and couldn't work anymore. Afternoons found her sitting in her favorite chair, sipping old-fashioned cocktails, watching the Million Dollar Movie on WOR-TV Channel 9 New York. The house was not as clean as it used to be, and she seemed blurry and short-tempered. But she didn't really get angry until she caught Allan in bed with me on the second day of his visit. She screamed and sent him packing, leaving me despondent and desperate to get back home.

At Grandmom's, the adults were acting surly; and looking back, I could understand why.

The year before the trip, 1972, we had moved from Brigantine to Ventnor. Dad was in financial straits. He had a loan on Grandmom's house to help finance our house on 29th Street, and he had stopped paying on it. Because of Dad's actions, Grandmom nearly lost her home (where generations of her family had lived since before World War I) to a sheriff's sale. Mom had racked up medical bills, and Dad was behind in payments on those as well. For our trip across country, he decided to buy a new station wagon and a brand-new camping trailer.

And now here we were, a family of six, descended upon Grandmom's house because Dad had again mismanaged money. Our trip was cut short because of it, and we couldn't go home yet because of the sublease. Mom and Dad argued constantly, and we teenage girls were noisy, hungry mouths to feed.

On the third day, Dad woke up to discover Mom had fled with the family station wagon back to Ventnor without us. Apparently the night before, they had received news that the tenants moved out, so they made plans to leave in the morning. But Mom changed that. Poor Dad had to enlist Uncle Doug to drive us back to Ventnor, where Dad picked up the station wagon, returned to Grandmom's, hooked up the trailer, and slunk back home to Ventnor. His first order of business was to sell back the trailer and downsize the car, trading in the family station wagon for a Zodiac Blue 1973 Delta 88 Royale.

Mom found a plastic baggie of marijuana left by the tenants in one of the kitchen cabinets above the refrigerator and became gleeful. That bag of pot was like the paper dress, young and modern; and she was determined to smoke it, harvest the seeds, and grow her own.

She found an empty flowerpot, filled it with soil and seed, and stuck it on the kitchen sill, right in the window where anyone walking by could see it. It sprouted, of course, and Mom was giddy with its progress. Lisa and Leslie admired it and pronounced Mom "cool," while I was dying inside and worried about narcotics officers breaking down the door and arresting us.

Furious, I threatened to throw the scraggly plant out. Mom saw I was serious, so she bought a grow light and hid the plant in the utility room. That little plant continued to defy the law and struggle upward, it's pointed, serrated leaves reaching out toward the bare bulb above. It wasn't on public display anymore; but every time I passed the utility room, I felt its malicious presence, capable of undoing us all.

On the day I finally grabbed the plant, stuffed it in a bag, and tossed it into a dumpster two blocks away, I felt vindicated and strong. Mom would scream at me, but I didn't care. What was she going to do, report me? Who could she call? She had no recourse, and maybe for the first time, I had the upper hand. I almost thought I was in control.

2012

BACK TO BRIGANTINE

If we're not willing to look back into the
past to find out the truth about what
happened, we really can't move into the
future with any hope for healing.

—James Talent

View from Rogge deck

By the time Lisa and I met at the Rogges' house in Brigantine in
August 2012, everyone was a suspect again, and I was exhausted from
running around in circles. I had reservations about accepting Lisa's

help. Obviously, she had her own motives. She wanted to be exonerated; I wanted the truth. Aunt Betsy wished we would just stop.

The Rogges both knew why I was there, and Betsy made it very clear she did not want to talk about the fire. It was too long ago. It was unpleasant. "Why would anybody want to open up that business again," Betsy said without a question mark.

We sat around their dining room table that overlooked the marshy bay between Brigantine and the mainland, where I spent years eating meals, doing homework, and daydreaming of a time I would live far away.

John and Betsy met at Columbia University when Betsy was just seventeen and one of the few girls attending the business school. John was working his way through college by serving tables in the women's dining room. Girls sat in the same assigned seats for each meal, and Betsy sat at one of the three tables John served. He was quickly smitten, but full of propriety. Betsy was so young; he couldn't just ask her out. But he did notice her fondness for eating pig tails, so he started saving them for her, slipping the little delicacies by ones and twos into a cotton handkerchief he kept in his pants pocket, whenever he found extras in the kitchen.

John said, "One time, I was standing in a subway train and had to sneeze." The way they both snickered here made us laugh, even on the eighth telling.

"Scattered all over the floor of that train," Betsy said.

"I got some stares that day," John said.

Lisa's younger daughter loudly whispered to her sister, "Why did she want pig tails?" The older girl shrugged and glanced at her mother, but Lisa was wrapped up in the story, laughing and looking only at Uncle John.

John was nearly blind and wore wraparound sunglasses most of the time. At ninety-two, his hearing was not a whole lot better than his eyesight, but he still walked every day and chatted with anyone who was inclined. He was a familiar sight out on the busy four-lane boulevard to the Brigantine Bridge, walking sure-footed if slowly to the island's only traffic circle, past the recently christened Mayor John Rogge Street, around the pharmacy where my mother helped me pick out supplies for becoming a woman and which now sold cheap souvenirs, beach umbrellas, and balls. John and Betsy still attended civic functions and community dinners. By this time, Betsy had accumulated decades of experience keeping conversations positive and light. She was a charming hostess and was still laughing lightly as she began telling the story of the kitchen in their first house, which John designed while she was in the hospital having their firstborn. There were no drawers in that kitchen—not one!

We couldn't persuade Betsy to talk about the fire, so we had to work around her. It occurred to me that Betsy might hesitate to speak ill of Lisa. After all, it was Lisa who became the good daughter, who visited every year with her daughters and attended church with them on every Sunday she was there. I knew that I could not come alone and ask the Rogges to talk behind Lisa's back. That's why it was crucial that Lisa and I came together and presented a united family front.

The next morning, I got up and ran five miles. In the early-morning moist coastal heat, I ran past the empty lot on 29th Street where our house used to stand and then past the jeweler's house where Mom would sneak off late at night. I showered at my hotel and returned to the Rogges. John and Betsy were sitting on the back deck watching the shore birds swoop and dive into the bay in search of breakfast. I sat with them and outlined our plans for the day. Lisa and I were going to talk to former city manager Jimmy Barber, who had been helping us ask around about the case. Then we had a meeting with the Ventnor Fire Department and afterward a visit with Maurie Cole in the county nursing home.

"I don't know why you need to dig this up now," Betsy said firmly. She had that worried look on her face.

"Well, I think it's about closure, and because it's not fair to Lisa, who has been a suspect all these years. Tomorrow, we have an appointment with the Atlantic County Prosecutor's Office," I told Betsy, hoping that she could at least be impressed with my resolve. She could see that I had a list and my plan for the day, so she nodded and turned her face back toward the bay where two seagulls were swinging wide and circling each other over the water.

It was nearly noon when Lisa slid into my rental car for the short ride back up the island to Andre's pizza place where we were meeting Jimmy Barber. Before we made the first turn, I told her about going back to the Waterview townhomes. I didn't know why. I was chatting about how the place looked now and how I couldn't find our old parking lot for the longest time. Lisa interrupted, "What was the name of the family across the way?"

"Family?"

"We went there, the night of the fire."

"You mean Kripitz? I went there, as soon as we got out of the house." I could see their front door as I said this. Mr. Kripitz was a businessman, recently divorced with a five-year-old daughter and three older sons. The middle son, Jeff, was in college in Florida but visited often; and I thought he was really cute. The night of the fire, I ran straight to their door in my baby-doll pajamas. Jeff answered the door and immediately gave me one of his shirts to put on and let me use the bathroom. The fire trucks were already there.

Lisa nodded. "Kripitz. You worked for him, right?"

"I cleaned house for him," I said. "And his sons who lived with him during the summer when they were home from college."

"I was just remembering," Lisa said. "You had keys to their house, and I used to go into your coat that was hanging in the closet and get the keys from your pocket. Then I would go over to their house and search through their medicine cabinets looking for drugs."

It's like she just sucker punched me in the solar plexus. I could practically see my light-blue ski jacket hanging in the front closet with keys in the pocket. I thought it was safe there, in my own house, with keys in my pocket entrusted to me. I never once looked in Mr. Kripitz's medicine cabinets, not even to clean. That was private. To snoop was an absolute violation of trust. To steal was far beyond that.

"What?" My mouth was dry, and I couldn't think of the other words I should use.

"No, I don't think I found anything." Lisa laughed a little. Her voice had gone round and girlish again. "Maybe allergy pills? I probably would have taken those. I would do anything back then."

"I never heard about this," I finally choked out.

"No, I guess I never told you," she said in a dismissive voice. "Here's Andre's restaurant."

Jimmy Barber was just inside the door, chatting with another table of men who looked like they came here every day for lunch. By the time we said our hellos and sat at a large round table in the front bay window, I was able to put the Kripitz incident in a locked compartment in my mind.

Jimmy had not changed in the nearly three years since I saw him last except that now he was wearing a tropical shirt, softly faded and worn. He said he was happy enough to be retired although he stayed active and kept in touch with his old law enforcement buddies from his days as an investigator in the county prosecutor's office.

Lisa and I agreed to share a cheesesteak sub and a green salad, while Jimmy ordered two slices of cheese pizza. I needed to remind him of the details of our case since he shredded all of his files upon his exit from the Brigantine City manager's office two years ago. He felt bad about the shredding, he said, since he knew he had done a little bit of poking around on his own and had some notes. When he didn't hear from me, he thought I lost interest.

"No, I was just making sure my daughter graduated college and was busy managing my real estate consulting business," I said with a smile. "You know how time can run away from you."

Jimmy chuckled and moved around some of the pieces of the police file that I'd put in front of him. One hand fanned and shuffled the papers, while the other hand poked a folded slice of pizza into his mouth.

"Yeah, here. This is the thing I remember from your file." Jimmy tapped a sheet of paper away from the others and turned it toward me with two fingers. "This I found curious."

I could tell at a glance which report that was, from the page formatting and the single paragraph of text. It's the document that reported Walter Buzby, arson investigator with the Atlantic County Prosecutor's Office, called and said to put the case on hold because he was about to "blow it wide open."

"Yes," I said. "It's proof that they were close to finding something."

"Well, I tell you I served with Walter Buzby in the prosecutor's office," Jimmy said, shaking his head. "Everyone called him Uncle Walt, and we all had the highest respect for him. He was the best arson investigator we had, and I learned a lot from him." Jimmy put down his slice and wiped his greasy fingers on a napkin. "There's no way he would have said something like this. No way at all. But the lieutenant detective who wrote this report, this crazy report saying that Uncle Walt wanted Fields to hold off on investigating? Let me tell you this lieutenant detective and Fields did not see eye to eye. You see what I'm saying?"

"It was a practical joke?" Lisa asked.

"I don't know if they were joking," Jimmy said. "And I can't say anything for sure because I didn't join the prosecutor's office until just after this. I'm just telling you that this lieutenant detective and Fields, they didn't work together too well."

"Oh," I said. Did he mean that the investigators weren't close to solving the case or just that he didn't trust the lieutenant?

"But I had another thought. All the investigators back then, we kept all of our notes on three-by-five index cards. It would help us when we were thinking about a case to shuffle the cards around and lay out the facts in different patterns. We might put things on our cards that we wouldn't put in official reports. I know Fields kept cards on his cases. He stored them in a metal filing cabinet. If you could get someone to give you the cards, you might find something new," Jimmy said and picked up another slice.

We went on through lunch, talking about who was still alive and who might have a phone number or a lead on various people who might be connected to the case. I told him about finding the former captain from the Ventnor Fire Department, the one who investigated our case, but who now had an advanced case of dementia. Jimmy remembered talking to Lisa's friend Beth a couple of years ago, but she didn't have anything new then and wasn't likely to now.

Lisa added she asked Beth and her friend Stuart if they remembered anything, but no luck. "Stu is still in touch with Joey C., who is dying of cancer in Florida now," Lisa said. Joey C. was the investigators' favorite suspect, and I would admit that I hoped for a death-bed confession. It seemed possible. It was surprising to me that Lisa kept in contact with so many neighborhood kids over the decades. Maybe they shared a secret, keeping it tight. The thought made me push my plate away.

Joey C. had the kind of tough life—addictions and self-made bad luck—that made a person think about karma and a guilty conscience. Lisa shook her head *no.* Nobody remembered anything. Nobody had any new information.

Lisa talked about the polygraph test she was given and being certain she failed. I saw the light in Jimmy's eyes disappear behind some kind of veil as she talked. I was not sure if he saw Lisa as the arsonist or someone to pity. Lisa sat back a little in her chair, pushed her plate away, and firebombed every last shred of good feeling I possessed.

"I'm just wondering about another thing," she said. "Back in the mid-1980s, I knew this guy who was renting a room from an older guy in Atlantic City. This guy, he told us that his roommate—the old guy—had a lot of cash stashed in his house. So, I mean, we were junkies, right? Another friend and I, we crept into his apartment when we knew he wouldn't be there; and we stole the money." Lisa held Jimmy in her laser focus; and I thought that, for her, I was not at the table at all. "It was twenty thousand dollars or something. Of course, we blew it in like three months; we were using heroin. But here's the reason I'm asking. You know how in twelve-step programs you need to atone for what you've done? Well, I know that the guy we stole from is dead now, so I can't tell him I'm sorry. And the statute of limitations is past on burglary. But I am wondering if you think it would be helpful if someone told the police that they could close the book on this case, that it was solved. You know, maybe do that anonymously?"

The veiled look on Jimmy's face hardened. He looked down at his hands and rolled a clean knife over and over on the red-and-white checkered vinyl tablecloth. Finally, he said that a case like that, outside the statute of limitations, would have been closed long ago. Nobody was worrying about it anymore, Jimmy said.

Lisa nodded like she expected as much. I busied myself paying the waiter for our lunch and thanking Jimmy for his time. I used every ounce of willpower I had to not bolt from the restaurant or bury my face in shame. I wanted Jimmy Barber to like us and help us. From the look on his face, I knew I shouldn't call him again. I wondered if he thought Lisa or one of her friends started the fire. It didn't seem useful to ask.

I dropped Lisa off at the Rogges without discussing her cat burglary past and drove across the Brigantine Bridge and through Atlantic City, thick with people and cars in the gray, smothering afternoon humidity, and headed back into Ventnor. The weather matched my mood.

At the stately red brick fortress that housed the thirty-eight-member Ventnor Police Department, there was a phone receiver hanging outside a locked door with a sign directing visitors to write a note and slip it into the wooden box if nobody answered the phone. I let the phone ring fifteen or twenty times before someone picked up.

The detective lieutenant was, once again, too busy to see me, a young officer said, just as the detective lieutenant had been too busy to take or return my calls for the past two years. "Leave a note," he said. In the note, I wrote that I was specifically looking for Detective Field's index cards on my case so that the detective would know I was not just fishing. But I had little hope he would call me back.

It was only a few short blocks to the fire department where two handsome young firefighters were making themselves an early dinner in a disheveled back room. They recognized my name, having taken messages from me a few times. The captain was, of course, busy. One of the young men slipped out a door to double-check, and I was struck nearly speechless when he returned with a pleasant-looking middle-aged man who stuck out his hand and introduced himself as Capt. James Culbertson.

Captain Culbertson had sympathy for me, but just didn't know what he could do. He remembered the Overton fire. His father actually fought that fire back in 1974 and told him about it, when the captain was younger. He took a personal interest and looked for the file, but never did find it.

"Did you hear that my sister was a suspect in the case?" I asked.

"I don't recall hearing that," Captain Culbertson said, scratching the back of his head. Then he held open the door and led me toward his truck so he could find a business card and see me on my way. "Now, the file might be up in the attic somewhere, and I suppose I could maybe crawl around up there and take a look," he said, squinting toward the fire department's high roofline. We stood at the curb for a bit, sweating and looking at the eaves, struck dumb by the mid-August heat. "Maybe in the cooler months," he said.

And anyway, the captain had been very busy lately. His father died a few years back. This year, it was his mom. Lately, he's spending a lot of time traveling up to sort through the house, cleaning out the accumulated decades of a family.

"Maybe one of your younger guys could go up into the attic looking for that file," I said hopefully, twinkling a smile and nearly winking at him.

"I wouldn't assign my men anything I wouldn't do myself," he said with finality.

I took one last long look at the fire department's eaves, thanked the captain for his time, and got back into the rental car. I thought this investigation would be like training for a marathon—lots of hard work, maybe a bit of a slog sometimes, but with the satisfaction of getting some miles under you. It was not. This was like running on a treadmill in a sweaty old gym, surrounded by people suggesting that you quit and go home.

*****

"I have to say one thing first; and that is, deep in your hearts, I think you girls know what really happened." Chuck DeFebbo, lieutenant and range master with the Atlantic County Prosecutor's Office, clasped his hands together and leaned forward with his forearms on the table, looking intently from Lisa to me and back again. "You just need to break through."

Lisa and I sat perfectly still across the conference table from DeFebbo—also an arson expert—and a solemn brunette victim-witness advocate named Kristin. The walls in that featureless conference room were close and beige; they seemed to be made out of some kind of sound-deadening tile. DeFebbo was a balding, husky man. He looked as though he surely played football in school, but not much since. I focused on the clasp of his strong hands so that I wouldn't stand up and slap that look of fake concern off his face.

My heart does not know anything, I wanted to say. *How about if we stick to the facts?*

I willed myself to keep silent. I was agitated and all too aware that Lieutenant DeFebbo was Lisa's ally. Was it two years ago that he told me on the phone that he and his friends were likely up to the same "pranks" that Lisa was at that age? I wanted to ask him if he ever stole twenty thousand dollars from the home of a friend and then lied about it for decades and then announced the fact over lunch with a former law enforcement officer as part of some twelve-step search for absolution.

No. I would not panic. I would not let my anger show. DeFebbo had told us that he had, essentially, the same information we had, with some photographs. I desperately wanted those photos as proof of arson.

The Atlantic County Prosecutor's Office had its own file, of course. "Uncle Walt" Buzby, the widely acknowledged guru of fire investigations in southern New Jersey, compiled it. But that file was destroyed after a water pipe burst in an off-site storage facility sometime in the 1980s. While I was busy having babies and building a real estate career on the other side of the country, the institutional memory of my parents' murder was disintegrating.

What DeFebbo had was a copy of the Ventnor Police Department file, with a dozen black-and-white photos of the fire's aftermath. He indicated that these eight-by-ten glossies survived the flood, but he did not know how. The photographs did not appear to have ever been wet. Also, notes in the file indicated the photographs taken were in color. It was a big deal in 1974 to have full color photographs. I didn't ask about the discrepancy.

"The detective in this case should have taken samples for accelerant testing right after the fire, and he did not," DeFebbo said as he laid out photos on the big laminate table. He made a perfect grid: four photos across and three down. Lisa and I leaned forward, studying the images. Within the silvery grays and blacks of the photos, dimly remembered pieces of furniture slowly emerged. I saw an exterior shot of the town house, and my stomach flipped over. The outside of the town house—brick on the bottom, clapboard on the second story, flat metal slab roof—was scarred black and looked like a news photo of Beirut after a bombing. The master bedroom window was a gaping black hole. The metal roof was melted and collapsed above my parents' window. The house looked like a bomb victim with half her face blown off. "Scientifically speaking, the methodology just wasn't as advanced in 1974," DeFebbo explained. "But we do know from the state lab that there were no added compounds. That means that there were no accelerants found at the scene."

"Are you talking about the piece of rug that was tested?" I asked.

"Yes. It tested negative," DeFebbo said.

"But those samples weren't collected until weeks after the fire. Isn't it possible the accelerant was dissolved or washed out by that point?" I asked.

"The tests are quite sensitive," DeFebbo said. "Trace evidence would still be found."

"But how can you conclude that there were no accelerants used when the only thing that was tested was a bit of rug collected weeks after the fact? And we don't even know where the piece of rug and foam backing came from," I said. "The pooling patterns were found in the living room. What if this rug sample was taken from somewhere else in the house?"

"That's true. We don't know that," DeFebbo said. He glanced quickly at Kristin, the victim advocate, who made a soothing sound; but she too was distracted by the array of photos lying on the table. He said, "There is a lot that we don't know."

Lisa had been quietly studying the images and pointed out a few things: the roll-top desk from the middle bedroom, right next to the window that she and Leslie jumped from, and a lighter spot on the wall where a bookcase once stood in the den. Then she tapped one of the photographs of the living room. It was all blacks and grays, a Rorschach test of the aftermath.

"Is this it?" Lisa asked, tapping the dark stain in the middle of the photo. "Is this the pooling pattern?"

DeFebbo slid his hands off the table and into his lap. "You know, there used to be all sorts of ways that charred scenes were interpreted. For instance, investigators used to look at spalling—a pattern left on concrete after a fire—and think it could tell them how a fire started. We know that isn't true now. What it looks like to me is that the fire started in the den, which had some pretty flammable paneling, the floor finished with a volatile compound. On top of that, the open-floor plan and all the open windows created a natural chimney. Essentially, the fire was free-burning for so long, with all the windows open, that it simply appeared to have an accelerant," DeFebbo said.

"But how did the fire start?" I asked, dizzy from this swarm of conflicting opinions.

"We will never know that, unfortunately, because your parents didn't make it," DeFebbo said, as if my parents were the only ones who might have the answer.

I asked DeFebbo for copies of the photos. He and Kristin exchanged an unreadable look. The case was still open, DeFebbo said, so he couldn't really share anything from the file. Nothing had happened with the case for thirty-eight years, he acknowledged, but the case was open because Lisa and I started asking questions. Our questions reopened the case, so now it was protected. But he said he was willing to ask.

DeFebbo and Kristin left the room, closing the door behind them. Lisa and I sat alone with the photos, staring dumbly at the collection. Where the living room rug used to be and flowing out from the center of the room toward one wall, there was a black pool of charred wood. I knew from the reports that this was a clear sign of malevolence. How could DeFebbo shrug it off?

Lisa murmured, "I don't know what to think." My brain felt like a series of locked gears. My stomach roiled at the sight of all that charred wood and twisted metal, and for a moment, I feared I was going to be sick. It was proof that the fire was real and not just my own demon. I was seventeen years old again and inside that burning house. The toxic funnel of smoke gathered around my head.

DeFebbo came back in the room, Kristin again in tow. He did not have an official reply to our request yet, but he promised to follow up. DeFebbo clasped his hands and put his forearms on the table again.

"Obviously, I cannot draw a conclusion as to how the fire started," he said. "When I drew up a diagram of the scene and compared it to Buzby's report, however, I did see fuels on-site and plenty of oxygen. Your mom had a history of suicide attempts and a blood alcohol level of 0.13 that night," DeFebbo's voice had become softer, almost apologetic, but unwavering. "We don't know whether that was her peak level, even. It could have been much higher. But there's something else. Your mom's carbon monoxide blood level was double that of your dad's. He was around 40 percent, and she was 80. That tells me she had more exposure to the fire. I think she might have been in the den smoking and maybe fell asleep. It could be that she tried to put the fire out and that she spent too long trying to do that. Or maybe she was trying to cover it up. I don't know. I just know that she had an extreme amount of exposure." DeFebbo shuffled through his file and pulled out the time log from the fire department. "And this really leaps out at me. Look at what your mom said when she made the emergency call. She said, 'Help me. The whole house is on fire.' *Me.* As if she was alone and discovered it."

Of course, I had considered the possibility that my mother—careless insomniac smoker—accidentally started the fire. Who wouldn't? But then, I went back to the conclusions of investigators like Uncle Walt, who decided there were "multiple points of origin" and "pooling patterns," and I was not sure what DeFebbo was trying to sell me.

"I also think, back at that time, people looked at Lisa's rebellious nature and made assumptions," DeFebbo went on. I leaned back in my chair, crossed my arms, and waited for it. This was what he wanted to sell. "But they did that—made assumptions about Lisa—based more on perception than actual fact. Frankly, I don't see anything in this file to indicate a real purpose to hurt you guys. I would like to think this was accidental," DeFebbo said. "And I think you know it, deep down."

Two or three sharp responses flew through my head, but my eyes fell back on the photographs, and I smiled instead.

"Thank you very much for your time," I said politely. "I look forward to hearing from you about getting copies of these photos."

DeFebbo stood, but then sat again quickly and placed all ten fingertips on the tabletop. "Look. I know that we're all here because of Uncle Walt's alleged statement to the lieutenant in Ventnor about blowing the case wide open," DeFebbo said. "But I know Uncle Walt well, and I know he would not have used those words or said that at all. He never would have tried to stop an investigation."

By the time we got back to Brigantine, I felt like I was falling backward and throwing wild punches as I went. Lisa and I managed to stop at the county nursing home in Northfield on our way back to the island, to talk to Maurie Cole. Lisa tried to wake him and get him to eat a little tepid applesauce from his lunch tray. But the most Maurie could do was nod his big, shaggy head on his thick neck and mutter to himself. He seemed like an ancient white-faced elk to me, chewing on some memory of grass and staring blankly into a dim forest. I doubted he knew we were there.

That evening, I tried to shake off my depression with another five-mile run through Brigantine, past the absent house on 29th Street, past a tiny street fair in front of the fire station consisting of a bounce house, four booths selling food and soft drinks, and a live band playing "Free Bird." I stopped at the liquor store where my parents had an account until Dad couldn't pay the bill anymore and bought a bottle of red wine to drink later in my hotel room. I hardly slept at all that night, chasing dead ends and ghosts. No matter how I tried to still my mind, I just kept seeing Lisa's teenage hands striking a match.

The next morning when I walked into the Rogges, Lisa took me by the arm. "Uncle John says they'll talk," she said. From the entry hall, I could see that Betsy and John were already sitting in the sunny dining room with Lisa's girls. I asked Lisa what changed, but she just shrugged and gave me a sly grin.

By the time I sat at the table, my single cup of coffee that morning felt like it turned into ten, burning a hole in my stomach. Betsy was lamenting she really thought us girls would have better uses for our time and energy than to rehash old events. She seemed anxious. Lisa asked her teenage daughters to go to the living room.

"Here's one thing you probably don't know," Betsy said. "Just a few weeks before the fire I remember, Nancy came here to see me about something. We talked a little about you girls, and she told me she was more worried about Leslie than Lisa. She said she was going to get some counseling for Leslie. I don't suppose that ever happened."

I shook my head slowly, and Lisa said, "I don't remember either of us getting any counseling then. Mom took me to a few sessions before that, when I was still in middle school. I remember because the therapist had these nuts in a bowl and I took one even though Dad told me not to touch anything, so he gave me a smack. Then the therapist asked me how that made me feel, and I was like 'What?' I did something wrong; I got hit. It never occurred to me to *feel* any way about it."

I looked over and saw Lisa was talking, but I could not really hear her words. We were finally all here, four years after I got the file and started asking questions. The Rogges would finally tell us the truth about the investigation. I didn't care about Lisa's therapy.

"Well, I'm wondering, Aunt Betsy, about something that we heard from Doug and Jill. We just wanted to know if you and Uncle John arranged to have the arson investigation stopped."

Aunt Betsy's eyes went dark and as round as cartoon eyes. Uncle John leaned forward in his chair and said, "What? What was that she asked?"

"We could not," Betsy sputtered indignantly.

"What?" John repeated.

"I'm asking if you asked the investigators, Walter Buzby and the others, to stop investigating our fire, so that it could be ruled an accident," I said a little too loudly. I just wanted to make sure that Uncle John heard me.

"Geez," Betsy breathed the word.

"No. Absolutely not," John said, pointing his face in my direction. "We could not have done that."

"That's what I said," Betsy said.

"That would have been illegal," John said. "And they wouldn't have listened to us anyway. Why would they?"

"Well, you were the mayor," I said, less sure of myself now. "And there was Maurie Cole and Senator Perskie with you too."

The corner of John's mouth twitched down hard, and for a second he looked like a stroke victim. "Those investigators wouldn't have listened to us if we had asked," he said. "And why would we? Why would we want the investigation stopped?"

"For the insurance money? For us I mean. There was double indemnity for accidental death so we got more money," Lisa explained.

We were so sure of this idea when we were all together at the Residence Inn in California. It made sense. But John and Betsy looked like we had insulted them.

"No," John said.

"It's ridiculous," Betsy said.

I was opening and closing my mouth like a fish, trying to think of some way to restart this conversation that had now gone horribly awry. What else did I want to know?

"I'll tell you what I remember, and that's the summer of 1974, when we kept getting called to go pick up Lisa at the police department for one thing or another," John said. "She got picked up in Ventnor for mooning the cops. Remember that?"

"Oh, yes," Betsy remembered. Together, she and John quickly piled up the stories: Lisa, the runaway, vandalizer, loiterer, pot smoker, and juvenile delinquent, cursing over the dishes, dropping the F-bomb, hitchhiking away from the house. "Another time, she brought this kid home. She came to me and said, 'Aunt Betsy, I brought this boy home; he's in my room, and you need to look at him because you're a nurse.' This boy was so yellow, his eyeballs were yellow, and he was so thin; he was a cadaver," Betsy said turning her chair toward Lisa. "I told you he had to go to the hospital and you kids were going to have to take him there. He was probably pop-ping drugs and used dirty needles, and that was it. You could feel the heat radiating off of him. They took him to the hospital, and he was dead three days later." Lisa was sitting straight in her chair, showing the kind of excellent posture we emulated from Aunt Betsy. But she looked fragile too, like a child facing a storm and trying not to be afraid. "As far as the cops were concerned, drugs were absolutely a part of that fire that killed your parents," Aunt Betsy was adamant. Lisa started to laugh, but Aunt Betsy kept talking a little louder. "Whether it was some drug dealer who was unhappy with you or somebody you promised drugs to but didn't deliver, that was the main connection with you."

"But I wasn't anything," Lisa cried out in her girlish voice, high and round. "I was just a low-level, pot-smoking, stealing-drugs-from-medicine-cabinets type of person. I wasn't selling. Well, maybe just to a friend. I might say, "Here, give me two dollars and I'll give you this black beauty," like that. I admit my boyfriend might have been doing that, selling, but he never took me along."

Lisa's voice pitched higher still, and she looked a little breathless, like a runner who had rounded a curve in the path to find a cliff. John, Betsy, and I started filling in her silence with other stories: Mom drunk at vacation Bible school and Dad selling the house on 29th with a different realtor. After all, we're family. When she was steady again, Lisa mentioned the fact that the Rogges delivered her to Jill and Doug that summer before the others. They made a special trip to get rid of her.

"You did the right thing, getting rid of me," Lisa said. "I would have done the same thing."

"Well, outside of killing you," Betsy said for the laugh.

"No. You did the right thing," Lisa insisted. There was a wet catch in her voice, and tears started rolling down her face. "There was no way to control me in this town. I knew where to go and how to get there. I would have just gone from garage to couch to beach to wherever. I was out of control. I wasn't going to listen to anybody, and you did the right thing sending me out of here. And I love you for it, Aunt Betsy. It makes me feel bad, thirty-eight years later, how badly I treated you. You loved me just because you loved me, not for any other reason. That has always meant the world to me, how good you were to me. In spite of how bad I was to you, you still gave me goodness. And that meant everything to me. When I thought later about how I wanted to be when I grew up and whom I wanted to be like and who had the values I most admired, it was you. You and your whole family. You did the right thing to get me out of here then."

2013

HALF TRUTHS, HALF SISTERS

If it's not one thing, it's your mother.
—Robin Williams

Drew, Age 6, circa 1994

There is a reason people say it's dangerous to poke around in the ashes of family secrets. You can choke on what gets stirred up. I had been home from Brigantine for about a week and was sitting in my

California backyard, feeling the first cool breeze of night sweep across the lawn, when my cousin Kim called from Florida. It was midnight in Florida, and I could practically hear the steam heat in her voice, along with the wine she had with dinner.

"Hey, so I was having dinner with Mom and Dad tonight and heard some pretty interesting things," Kim began, running a few of the words together.

I laughed lightly and said, "What's that?"

"You have to promise not to tell," Kim said.

"Okay," I answered, feeling noncommittal about this promise.

"You can never tell Dad I told you."

"Okay."

"Well, he told me tonight that you are not your father's daughter."

"What?"

"Dad said that Frank was not your real dad," Kim spit out with a rush of excitement. "Your mom told him that, a long time ago. She said you weren't Frank's daughter."

My first thought: *Of course*. My stomach felt ripped in half, but I was not surprised. I knew the truth of this statement instantly.

People always said I was different from my sisters. We all looked like my mother. But I was more energetic and had remained thin without trying too hard. I was more conservative in my habits and appearance. Uncle Doug said it more than once: *I was different from my sisters*. I felt my pulse throbbing in my head and then became aware that Kim was still talking.

"He doesn't want you to start looking," Kim cautioned me.

"Who?" I asked. "What?"

"Dad. He told me not to tell you because he didn't want you to go looking around for your real father," Kim repeated.

"How does he know this?"

"Your mom told him, back when you were still living in Fords," Kim confided with a hushed quickness. She was enjoying the drama of the moment. "I guess she told Aunt Millie too."

Millie was not a true aunt, but one of my mom's oldest friends and Lisa's godmother. According to Kim, both she and Uncle Doug heard the same story: Mom went down to Atlantic City for training sessions with the phone company where she worked, met a man in a bar, and came back pregnant. I guessed I could track down Aunt Millie without too much trouble and ask a few questions. But I wondered what I really wanted to know. The man who raised me was my dad. What else was important?

Who killed my dad?

Who was my dad?

"I just thought you would want to know for medical reasons, you know," Kim reminded me.

I opened my mouth, but could only imagine puking. I closed it again and took a big gulp of the cool, dry night air in through my nose. Immediately I thought, *I am in California. They can't really get me.*

When Kim referred to "medical reasons" for needing to know my lineage, she was talking about my son. Drew was twelve years old when he died of Duchenne muscular dystrophy.

Duchenne muscular dystrophy is a terrifying, terminal illness, and it is hereditary. Mothers are the carriers. We searched our family history and found no one from whom the disease could have been inherited, so I did some research. On the Muscular Dystrophy Association website, it says that DMD is only passed on the X chromosome, which comes from mothers. Fathers pass on Y chromosomes to their sons. But a father with DMD can pass the X to a daughter, and that daughter becomes a carrier. Any of her sons have a 50 percent chance of developing the disease. Or a mother can have a mutation in her egg cells and pass the disease on to her son that way.

When Drew was diagnosed, we all worried about my sisters' children and who else among us besides me might be a carrier. But only Lisa went through the expensive genetic testing to find out, because she was in the Navy and pregnant with her oldest at the time. Her tests came back negative. If I was a bastard, Kim knew I might be the aberration. Maybe my sisters and their daughters were safe from being carriers.

The next morning, I called Leslie and Lisa. I already selected a DNA testing lab that would send me collection kits, perform comparative testing, and have the answer back in a week or two. I just needed to get my sisters to agree to the cheek swab. I called Leslie first.

"Sure, of course I will," Leslie said and then laughed a little, a he-he-he that I recognized as disbelief. "Just incredible. I mean it wasn't enough that Mom was a crazy drunk, right? She had to be a cheater too."

Lisa told me, "If you're paying for it, I don't mind. Who knows? Maybe we're all from different fathers."

I did not call Liz after all. I knew just enough about DNA statistics to know that if I was full sisters with Leslie and Lisa, I was with Liz too. She did not need to be bothered. So I pushed the long-handled cotton swab along the inside of my cheek and sent it off to the lab and forgot about it. I was busy petitioning the state of New Jersey for copies of the fire photographs, so I had nearly forgotten Kim's secret when I opened an envelope from an address that looked vaguely familiar. I pulled out a sheet of paper with columns of undecipherable numbers. A short summary at the bottom explained the lab results.

Alleged sisters 1 and 2—that's me and Leslie—had a combined siblingship index of 0.0643, the report stated, making our probability of being full siblings just 6 percent. I choked and tasted bile in the back of my throat. This was absolutely wrong. *I must be reading these numbers wrong*, I thought. I was reading too fast. I didn't know this math.

I grabbed my cell phone and dialed the number for the lab in North Carolina. A man with a foreign accent patiently explained the numbers. Leslie was almost certainly my half sister, he said; our blood told my mother's secret. "But turn to the next page," the lab technician encouraged me. This was better news. See here? Lisa and I had a combined siblingship index of 161. To a 99 percent probability, Lisa was my full sister.

I thanked the man on the phone and sank numbly into a chair. What the hell was going on with Mom? Daughters 1 and 3 were with the same man, but daughter 2 was different. Who knew about daughter 4 now? If there was a man in Atlantic City, as the rumor went, did Mom go back for a second go-round after Leslie was born?

Was he the real reason we moved south? Was it a huge love affair? Did Nancy ever love Frank, or was he just her convenient enabler?

In Mom's letter to Grandmom, September 1969, she said she remade her vows to Dad after an unpleasant confrontation with her therapist and him. Maybe that meant Mom came to love Dad or found some redemption in acceptance.

Wait. Was the jeweler my father?

Jessica said I should start looking for "my sperm donor" right away. My daughter was a recent college graduate, living with me while she started her first real job, and had arrived at the age of certainty.

"I'm serious. These people aren't getting younger, and your father could be anybody," she said with a bit too much glee.

"You know, I think I'm a little tired of family right now," I answered.

"Maybe you have half sisters or brothers out there," she said, laughing. "Maybe there's—"

"Enough." I barked the word at her and was immediately sorry, but I could feel this anger growing and taking shape, becoming solid and starting to speak for itself.

My entire childhood was a lie. I used to think it was merely tragic. Now it was a cesspool of secrets that finally exploded when our windows blew out that hot night in 1974.

My closest sibling, Leslie, was not my full sister. Only my polar opposite, Lisa, shared my blood. After a lifetime of being locked in oppositional orbits, I was forced to see now that Lisa and I were far more alike than we were different. We were the two strongest personalities in the family, always responding to our own inner drives instead of majority opinion. While in Brigantine with Lisa, hearing about one ugly theft or lie after another, I had begun to imagine her once again as the arsonist. But now that seemed impossible. We shared the same blood, and cold-blooded murder was not within our DNA sequence.

Despite what I barked at Jessica, I also knew that I could not let this go. I did not like uncertainty. I called the lab again in North Carolina, ordered yet another test, and prepared to confront Liz—to coax, cajole, challenge, whatever it took. It was Leslie—now odd sister out—who did the convincing. She simply said to Liz "You owe me this" and did not explain what she meant to the rest of us. Liz opened her mouth for the swab.

After an agonizing two weeks, the same technician called to apologize in a singsong voice. "I am so sorry to tell you that there were errors in the original testing. In truth, it appears that you are the only half sister. The others are all full matches."

I took the information and stored it somewhere in my internal mainframe for a few days. I didn't talk about it. I didn't tell my sisters. I read the report and the columns of numbers verifying my new identity as a bastard.

Then, somehow, an amazing lightness started to accumulate in my periphery. I was buoyed, lifted up. I felt like a boat that had slipped its anchor line. I was unmoored and gloriously so. I spent a long weekend cleaning every closet in my house. I reminded Jessica, once again, the rules that should be applied when deciding whether to keep an item or throw it out. For no good reason, I felt hopeful.

At the end of the long weekend, I made phone calls and gave my sisters the updated genetic news. I sent them the DNA reports proving that I was the odd sister out.

The confusion that surrounded the DNA testing now mixed with questions about our family history. Mom and Dad were married almost three years before Mom got pregnant with me. With whom did Mom have an affair? Did she tell Dad, then or ever, that I was not his? Was Dad like Joseph of the Bible, volunteering to spare Mom shame and embarrassment by raising me as his own? Did Mom have three more kids with Dad to allay her guilt? The questions kept coming, but answers did not. But, in some ways, it didn't concern me for long, because I was the boat that slipped its anchor line.

I am only half Overton. But Overton is my father's name, and he is the only family member with whom I do not share DNA, so perhaps I can say that I am not Overton at all.

2014

WRONGFUL ACCUSATIONS

People who escape fatal fires with their lives may
face a tangle of emotions, fear, regret, relief…
If you survive a fatal fire, you have a very good
chance of being charged with setting it.
—John J. Lentini

Months slid past while I told myself that I didn't care anymore who
started that fire. I wasn't really an Overton. What business was it of
mine? I might have even believed that line for some fifteen-minute
period. But then late one afternoon, I was returning home from running errands; and halfway down the block, that smell was suddenly
everywhere—wood and plastics and hot, high heat all fused together,
coating the inside of my mouth and the back of my throat. I rolled
down my window, and the cloying smell invaded the interior of my
car. In the time it took to inhale, I was transported back to my fire
all over again.

Just ahead, a column of black smoke, dancing against the blue
sky like a live black cobra, came into view. I drove home quickly,
pulled into my garage, and rushed into the house. It was quiet and
cool from the air conditioning—empty. My heart was still hammering as I jammed my feet into a pair of running shoes and took off
down the street to find the source of the smoke. As I turned the corner, I was back in my fire scene: The street was filled with a big ladder truck, ambulances, and a couple of smaller fire trucks. I noticed
many of my neighbors standing stiffly in shock. Approaching the

burning house, I was transfixed by the flames I could see licking out the top of a second-story window. And suddenly more flames were burning on the roof next door. It wasn't just one house on fire but two. Firefighters swarmed everywhere, armed with hoses, dressed in full gear, sweating in the summer heat. It was at least ninety-five degrees out there and hotter with every step I took toward the house. A stream of water knocked the orange flames down from the second-story window. I blinked and looked away. One of my neighbors pointed out the woman who lived in the first house that was ablaze.

"Is anyone inside?" I called to her.

The woman turned a blank face to me, and I recognized the mask of shock. She shook her head; and then, as if just remembering the house was hers, she shouted for help to get her belongings out of the fire. One of the firefighters stood by her front door as some of us ran up and joined her. He directed us, and soon I was part of the caravan carrying pictures and small pieces of furniture out of the house to a neighbor's garage for storage. Then I pulled out my phone and took a few pictures. I didn't know why. I learned later that no one was in either house at the time of the fires, but a family pet did not make it out of one.

That same day or maybe the next, the mail brought another fire story. A friend who knew I was struggling with the meaning of evidence in my own case sent a magazine article about a man and his children and a mysterious house fire that plunged me right back into doubt. And it filled me with shame too, because when you considered his story, our story became a little less tragic.

Cameron Todd Willingham woke up coughing in a cloud of smoke, just like my sisters and I did, journalist David Grann wrote in *The New Yorker*. This happened in Corsicana, Texas, in 1991, two days before Christmas. Willingham was just twenty-three years old, but already had three little girls—a two-year-old named Amber and one-year-old twins Karmon and Kameron—and when he woke up from a nap into the dark-gray cloud that day, he immediately began yelling for his babies.

He ran shirtless out the front door onto the porch, screaming to neighbors that his babies were burning up. Willingham broke a window to get into the girls' room, but the flames shot straight out at him. The rest of the windows exploded soon after. When the firemen arrived, they found Willingham in hysterics and immediately started shooting water at the flames. Firemen in special gear tried to get in, but the flames knocked them back a couple of times. Finally, one firefighter in an oxygen mask was able to run in through where the front door used to be. Long minutes later, he emerged from the house carrying Amber's tiny body. The smaller girls were dead on the bedroom floor. Willingham's wife was not in the house at the time.

Corsicana's assistant fire chief—a man with twenty years' experience who said that fires spoke to him—and a deputy fire marshal, considered one of the state's top arson investigators, examined the scene. These were respected men. And for me, the story became a familiar litany of facts. There were deep char patterns on the floor and low on the walls of the hallway. Inside the girls' room were pooling patterns on the floor from a liquid accelerant, and the fire there was so intense that the metal springs under the children's beds turned white from the radiant heat. It seemed as though the floor had burned hotter than the ceiling, which was unnatural in light of the rule that heat would rise, investigators noted. They found glass that was still in a sheet, but shot through with fine, tight cracks. They called that crazed glass, a sign that the temperature had accelerated suddenly, investigators reported. This was no slow burn. It was a sudden, intense fire. The investigators found multiple points of origin.

How could someone choose to burn little girls? What kind of monster wanted babies dead?

Willingham was not a completely upstanding citizen. A high school dropout and out-of-work mechanic, he drank too much and liked heavy metal music. A tattoo of a skull and snake covered his left bicep. On a few occasions, Willingham hit his wife. He insisted, however, that he and his wife both loved the girls and that he had tried desperately to save them. He recalled crawling down the hallway on his hands and knees, first into the girls' room and then out the front door.

That would be the detail that killed him. The investigators had seen enough fires to know that puddling patterns in the hallway meant an accelerant was used and the floor would have been on fire. Willingham could not have crawled across the burning hall. Willingham insisted that the walls were on fire up high, near the ceiling. When he stood up in the girls' room after trying to feel around on the floor for the babies, his hair caught fire. The fire was high, he said, not low. But those pour patterns on the floor convinced investigators otherwise.

Within the month, Willingham was arrested and charged with the murder of his three daughters. Both Willingham and his wife insisted on his innocence, but at his death penalty trial, investigators systematically took jurors through the facts: the crazed glass, the puddles of charred floor, and the classic V patterns etched out in soot on the walls that clearly pointed to multiple points of origin. The only answer was arson. And who else could have possibly wanted those innocent babies dead than the man who was present and the fire's only survivor?

At trial, the state proved that Willingham poured lighter fluid from the front door of the 975-square-foot house through the living room, down the hallway, and into the children's bedroom. As he was retreating, he lit a match. It was a classic arson case with the pour patterns and burn trail. A jailhouse informant who said Willingham confessed was also presented to the jury. Willingham denied talking to the man and turned down plea deals that would have given him life in prison instead of the death penalty all the while insisting upon his innocence.

Willingham's wife testified that even though he had hit her, he never hurt the children. She refused to believe the state's theory that her husband was a sociopath who murdered his children in order to have more time to drink beer and play darts. Willingham was sentenced to death.

For thirteen years, Willingham sat in prison. His court-appointed lawyer filed the usual appeals, but made it clear that he did not believe in Willingham's innocence. "There were no grounds for reversal, and the verdict was absolutely the right one," defense attorney David Martin later told journalist David Grann. "Shit, it's incredible that anyone's even thinking about it."

Finally, someone very serious started thinking about it. In January 2004, one month before Willingham's scheduled execution, an anti-death penalty activist who befriended Willingham sent his case to Dr. Gerald Hurst. An explosives expert, chemist, fire investigator, and acclaimed scientist, Dr. Hurst invented Liquid Paper and Mylar balloons. During his career, he also conducted dozens of experiments with fire, publishing the results and pushing arson investigations closer to a science than an art. Instead of relying on intuition or anecdote, Dr. Hurst recreated specific conditions, set fires, and noted the results.

Four years earlier, Dr. Hurst had proved that a North Carolina woman who faced the death penalty in the arson murder of her seventeen-month-old son was factually innocent. Faulty wires set the blaze, not her.

Point by point in the article, David Grann explained how Dr. Hurst took apart the evidence against Willingham. State investigators said the melted aluminum front-door threshold was proof of an accelerant since the metal would not burn otherwise. Dr. Hurst pointed out that an ordinary wood fire could reach 2000 degrees Fahrenheit, while aluminum would melt at 1200 degrees. No accelerant was needed. Then there was the matter of crazed glass, which everyone said happened when glass met with sudden high heat—like from an accelerant fire—except, during the aftermath of the Oakland Hills fires in 1991, another science-minded fire investigator named John Lentini inspected more than fifty homes ravaged by brush fires and discovered crazed glass. It turned out that all those fine, closely spaced cracks happened when glass was cooled quickly, such as when firefighters sprayed water to put out the fire. A sudden burst of heat didn't create crazed glass at all.

The pour patterns, the burn trail—it was the result of flashover, not a flammable liquid. Based on the evidence, Hurst had little doubt that the fire was accidental most likely caused by the space heaters or faulty wiring.

The words on the page blurred. I realized I had stopped breathing. The evidence of arson in the Willingham case was the same as the evidence in the Overton case.

Pour patterns were not proof of liquid accelerant? What about splash marks on the bedroom threshold of a teenage girl? Experts said those were clear signs of murderous intent. Now, they were saying it was the result of flashover? I turned back to the article.

A year prior, continued the journalist Grann, a man named Gerald Wayne Lewis was charged with setting his house on Lime Street, in Jacksonville, Florida, on fire. Six people perished in that blaze, including Lewis's wife and four of his children. Again, investigators noted the classic signs of arson: low burns along the walls and floors, pour patterns and puddle configurations, and a burn trail running from the living room into the hallway. Lewis claimed the accidental fire began as a result of his son playing with matches in the living room.

The prosecution hired John Lentini and John DeHaan, another well-known arson scientist and author of fire investigation textbooks. In what became known as the Lime Street experiment, these experts procured the condemned house next to Lewis's. They duplicated the furnishings and wall coverings that had burned in the Lewis house and set the house on fire, without using an accelerant. Within four minutes, the house was engulfed. When the fire was investigated, they found charring along the base of the walls and doorways and, burning under furniture, a V-shaped pattern some distance away from where the fire had started—all the same conditions that were assumed to be the result of an accelerant fire.

The experiment provided the necessary reasonable doubt, and the charges against Lewis were dropped. I wondered how many death sentences Lewis would have received had the prosecution not hired those experts.

In the Willingham case, Dr. Hurst wrote his report and delivered it to an advocate who filed it with the state of Texas. The report was received, but there was no evidence that anyone really read it or considered its conclusions. On February 17, 2004, Willingham's appeals ran out. That night, the state of Texas executed Cameron Todd Willingham by lethal injection. His last words were "I am an innocent man convicted of a crime I did not commit. I have been persecuted for twelve years for something I did not do. From God's dust I came, and to dust I will return, so the earth shall become my home."

I put the article down. Everything I believed was being turned inside out. In the days that followed, I read everything I could find on the Internet about the new fire investigation techniques. I came up with another tragic case, Kristine Bunch.

At the age of twenty-one, Kristine was accused of setting fire to her trailer home, a blaze which killed her three-year-old son. She was convicted by a jury in 1996, receiving concurrent sentences of fifty years for arson and sixty years for murder. At trial, the same conditions that investigators found in our fire were used as evidence that Kristine had committed arson. The determination was the fire started in two locations with a liquid accelerant.

In prison, Kristine filled her time by completing her education and working to find a legal avenue out of her nightmare. Finally, after serving seventeen years, Kristine was released when the evidence against her was debunked by the experts.

A recent article by Megan Fernandez, in the January 2014 *Indianapolis Monthly*, asked, "When will Kristine Bunch be free?" Life after prison with no restitution from the state of Indiana, strained family relationships, mounting debt, and loss of freedom for so many years took a tremendous toll. Reading her story, my sense of despair and outrage mounted. How could this happen? And what if this had been our family? I turned back to the pages of my report, looking for common language or glaring anomalies and thinking about Mom and Dad.

When we were at the Atlantic County Prosecutor's Office with Lieutenant DeFebbo in 2012, he had mentioned something about advances in fire science. Just the thought of DeFebbo made me angry again, with his talk about opening my heart to see the truth. But I couldn't stop thinking about it. DeFebbo said that even though Buzby was a good investigator, the fire science had changed and his theories were not really valid today. In New Jersey, I dismissed that as a hedge. Now, I began to believe it as truth.

I called Lisa.

"I'm rethinking the book," I said quickly, before I could change my mind.

"Oh."

"Yes, I want to reinvestigate the fire, and I need your help. What do you think?"

"I don't know how to help you," Lisa answered in that neutral tone of hers.

"I'm just... I'm not convinced that it's arson anymore," I explained. I waited for a sound from her but heard nothing. "I've been reading about these new fire investigation techniques, and I think we need to find the people who know this stuff and have them review the case file. What do you think?"

"Okay," Lisa agreed. "But I don't know anyone who can do that."

"Well, neither do I; but you are really good at finding stuff on the Internet, and I thought we could start searching there, for people who know this stuff." There was silence on the line. Why wasn't she more excited about this? There I was, having a damn epiphany; and Lisa, who claimed that being called a teenaged parent-killing arsonist just about ruined her life, was dead calm. "Think about it, Lisa. How cool would it be if we could actually close the case and prove that you didn't do it?"

"I didn't do it," Lisa said without hesitation. "I know that I didn't do it, and that's all that really matters. But *you* still think I did it?"

Now it was my turn to be quiet. The middle school principal said she probably did it. Then there's the failed lie detector test, the criminal defense attorney, the drugs, and running away. For so long, I weighed these facts against Lisa. I wasn't entirely sure that I knew how to stop. I took a deep breath.

"I want someone with today's knowledge and expertise to tell us what really happened," I finally spoke. "I don't trust the work that was done by the Ventnor police detectives and fire investigators. Detective Fields just wanted to pin this on you or one of your drug-dealing friends. So, for me, I'm still where I was forty years ago not knowing the answers. But I think there might be someone out there who can help us."

Lisa promised to think about it.

A few days later, I read in my local newspaper that fire investigators determined that rags soaked with linseed oil and stored in my neighbor's garage had burst into flames, causing their fire. One house was a total loss; the other was just badly damaged. I was relieved, anyway, that the family knew what happened.

And then I went looking for the fire investigators mentioned in David Grann's story.

I searched for John Lentini and found that he was still in business as a fire investigator in Florida. According to his website, Lentini conducted more than two thousand fire scene inspections and wrote numerous articles about the "mythology of arson investigations" and "instinct giving way to modern science." I sent a letter asking for his help with our case. If someone with his knowledge could just review the reports I thought, surely it would help break up this dam of conflicting facts in my head, and the truth would become clear. I never heard back. When I finally got the courage to follow up by phone, he quickly dismissed me. The case was too old and the information too sparse to review, he said. "There is little use," he said, "and you would be better off getting a psychic to solve the case or waiting for someone to confess." I knew how to accept defeat by then, so I quickly thanked him and hung up.

John DeHaan, the other investigator mentioned in *The New Yorker* article, was also actively working cases. On a number of websites, I read about DeHaan's investigations and experience. He's the author of *Kirk's Fire Investigation*, a textbook in use today. The best part was that he was local. I quickly grabbed the phone and called him before my courage failed.

A few days later, a man with a scratchy voice called back and agreed to meet with me before he started teaching his next fire investigation class. I gathered up all my files, notes, and photos and drove to Vallejo.

2014

MEETING WITH JOHN DeHAAN

What you lose in the fire, you
will find amongst the ashes.
                        —French proverb

John DeHaan met me in the building lobby. A large man, he was casually dressed in khakis and a slightly wrinkled, short-sleeved dress shirt embroidered with his company logo. Looking at his pale eyebrows, I wondered how many times they had been scorched. His manner was easy-going, and I found myself immediately trusting him. I tried to imagine him as a firefighter but couldn't and settled on an image of a genial, slightly distracted college professor. Through narrow hallways, I trailed him to his office, so small and cramped that it looked like a fire hazard to me. From the floor on up, every imaginable surface was piled high with papers, file folders, photos, and books. John carefully cleared a space, and we settled in.

We talked for almost an hour and a half about the fire and the investigation. I told him that I contacted John Lentini, who told me that I either needed someone to confess or a psychic. John laughed and told me good luck with that—whether finding a confessor or a psychic I wasn't sure. I said, "I don't want luck, just your expert opinion." Now it was his turn to smile.

John's hands were in constant motion, fiddling with pens and papers on his desk, making buildings with his palms and fingers, as he talked about his early career. Like other firefighters, he was taught to *read* fires, to think of them in mystical and poetic terms. They looked for signs of heat intensity and burn patterns on the floor. He received a grant to study fires on his own. He followed the work of other investigators, and by the time the smoke was clearing from his umpteenth fire, he knew that just about everything he had been taught was wrong.

Arson fires are big business; arson is the leading cause of fires in the United States with direct property losses of almost two billion dollars. Investigators like John DeHaan, Gerald Hurst, and John Lentini have made great strides toward separating arson from accident; but it is still not uncommon for a fire to be poorly investigated or misinterpreted. Sherlock Holmes once said, "Insensibly one begins to twist facts to suit theories, instead of theories to suit facts."

John was doing a lot of intense and important work, changing the tide on an entire belief system in law enforcement, but he also seemed genuinely interested in my case as he asked me about the weather that day of the fire. Could I get a weather report for June 21, 1974? And the construction of the townhome, could I get building specifications? We talked about the on-off button for the Magnavox TV known for starting fires. He considered the television an ignition source and mentioned that it was one of the first fire targets identified by the Consumer Product Safety Commission back in the 1970s.

I remembered being asked by detectives what model television we owned. In fact, on June 1, 1974, the Consumer Product Safety Commission issued guidelines for television receiver safety. It was a two-page document, and item #13 referred to "instant-on," a feature that allowed sound and picture to come on as soon as the television's power button was touched. It meant the set would have an electric current passing through it at all times so it could be standing by to spring into action. Commissioners suspected the feature caused at least one fire; and they recommended that it be disabled by turning the defeat switch, also known as the vacation switch, to off.

We talked about Dad's refinishing projects as well—the hope chest for me, dad's old roll-top desk for himself—and John agreed to review my case based on the files I had. In addition, hadn't I mentioned some photographs? My shoulders dropped. The Atlantic County Prosecutor's Office would not release them to me, I explained.

I had asked nicely. I had petitioned the court and gone through a mediation process that took more than a year. I was denied. I asked if he knew anyone at the county prosecutor's office. He didn't, but agreed to reach out and said he worked with law enforcement all the time. Usually they cooperated since he would close their cases. I gave him Detective Chuck DeFebbo's contact information. John gave me the textbook he wrote: *Kirk's Fire Investigation, Sixth Edition*. It was heavy in my hand, and I left his office determined to read every word.

I hurried back to my car, phone in hand, and called Lisa. John agreed to take this case but needed more information, I blurted. With my real estate consulting business hitting overdrive, I really needed help. Lisa agreed and started taking notes while I read from the list of John's must-haves: a weather report from the day of the fire, floor plans of the townhome to see the layout, and construction specifications if we could get them, so that he could see what materials were used to build the unit. Lisa said no problem. I told Lisa she was the best and hung up the phone, my mind already jumping ahead to my next meeting of the day.

True to her word, Lisa began sending emails with answers a few hours later, while I was still in business meetings. She found the floor plan for our four-bedroom townhome at Waterview. She talked to the manager, Kathy Kosher, who was very helpful with finding the condo's master deeds; and she had offered to speak with our inspector if he needed more information.

Next, Lisa contacted someone at the Ventnor city building department to obtain the construction documents. After five years, a clerk told Lisa the policy was to send them to storage. At first, the clerk said that Lisa needed to get an Open Public Records Act (OPRA) request; and then she said, "Hold on. You'll have to contact the architect because the plans were copyrighted." In her email, Lisa included the link to OPRA, which described what information was available and how to get a record. I was already familiar with this frustrating process in trying to get photographs of the fire scene from the Atlantic County Prosecutor's Office. I told Lisa I thought we should pass on this path for now.

Lisa talked to the librarian at the *Press of Atlantic City*, Martha Zechman, to get a copy of the newspaper articles about the fire. Martha explained that most of that stuff was on microfilm and not available unless you actually went to the Atlantic City Library on Tennessee Avenue. I told Lisa not to worry about it, since I thought I already had copies of all the newspaper articles from our last visit.

The weather report was sent as reported by the National Climatic Data Center Global surface summary of the day for June 21, 1974. The high was 89.1 degrees Fahrenheit with a low of 70 degrees Fahrenheit and mean temperature of 78.5 degrees Fahrenheit with no rain, 0 percent precipitation, and a mean wind speed of 11.85 mph. I was surprised there was any wind reported at all, as I remembered the night as sweltering without a breeze.

In Lisa's last email of the day, she wrote, "My work is done here unless you give me a new assignment. And I'll send you an invoice for $250 worth of research so far. Just kidding."

I sent all the information off to John, hoping he could finally resolve the case. My balloon was immediately punctured when he emailed back to say what he really needed was the photographs from the fire scene. I wanted to shake my computer monitor in frustration. The prosecutors couldn't release the photos because it was an open case. It was an open case because Lisa and I had asked questions about it. There was no clear path to closing the case and making the photos available.

I asked John what to do, and he promised to make some calls to see whom he might know in New Jersey law enforcement. Barring that, he might just call Lieutenant DeFebbo. In the end, I wrote a letter to Lieutenant DeFebbo with John's help; and miraculously, ACPO sent the photographs from the case file to John.

In early September 2014, John sent me his report. He concluded that our fire was "probably the result of accidental ignition of upholstered furniture in the den by a dropped cigarette or match. There was no reliable evidence of an intentionally set fire."

Of course, by then I knew this was probably going to be the answer. But that knowledge did not beat back the sadness. I had spent forty years of living with a story about arson, about someone creeping around our house that night and trying to kill us. It was never true. I found myself grieving all over again and emotionally exhausted. I was so sad for Mom and Dad because maybe this tragedy could have been prevented.

I sent the report to my sisters and waited.

Lisa responded first. In an email, she said she was very happy. She wrote that she was full of emotion, thankful to me, and she probably owed Mom an apology for suspecting Mom of having started the fire for all these years. I got hung up on that for a moment, because I thought Mom *did* start the fire if it was her cigarette smoldering in the sofa. It was just accidental instead of arson. So I couldn't imagine why Lisa owed Mom an apology. I wished Aunt Jill were still alive. I would make sure she saw the report exonerating Lisa. I wanted her to know Lisa was innocent. I guess I did have a few regrets after all.

2014

The Truth Emerges

Veritati ex cinerarum.

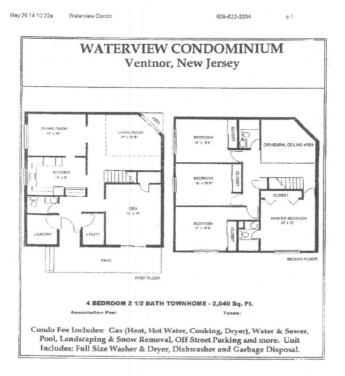

Waterview condo floor plan (mirror image)

In October 2014, my sisters and I agreed to meet with John at the Szechuan Chinese Cuisine restaurant on Solano Avenue near his office in Vallejo so he could explain his report to everyone and show us the photographs of the fire that only he could obtain. The traffic from the East Bay where I drove from delayed me; and my sisters and John were deep in conversation, gathered around a circular table at the back of the restaurant, when I arrived.

"I've gotten thrown out of restaurants before," John was saying. "I was telling my class the other day about it. I was with a group of European forensic investigators in Lisbon, and we were drinking brandy. In my defense, it was terrible brandy. We were really bored, waiting for the music to start. We each had tablespoons, and we were testing the ignition point of the brandy against the table candles. The waiter threw us out…"

Everyone was laughing as I apologized for being late.

"Oh, no worries," my sisters and I greeted each other. The remaining open seat at the table was offered to me. I noticed John had his textbook open, and as I sat down, he resumed talking.

"…This is a kitchen fire, and it's been ignited by overheating the oil on the stove. At this point, the stove has ignited the cabinets; and the fire is spreading through the hot smoke layer from the cabinets toward the door, which is the ventilation point. This is the onset of flashover. The whole room is filled with flames at the ceiling level, and now the radiant heat is igniting everything else in the room, including whatever floor covering there is; and now it becomes ventilation driven. Now the most intense part of the fire is at the door, where all the fresh air is rushing in. Now that the glass sliders have failed, that's what happened in that den. Flashover is something of a landmark. What happens in flashover is that you have a huge plume of flame coming out of any available ventilation openings, and at your house, it was coming out the den door and spreading out into the hallway."

I could picture John in front of a class of eager college students, explaining fire science from his textbook, fielding questions as he taught.

"How could you see that?" someone asked.

John closed the textbook. "I'll show you in the pictures," he answered, "but basically the key is to understand how fires are going to spread in a multi-compartment building. I started with the floor plan. Thanks to the contributions of you girls, we had descriptions of the furnishings and where things were. And so what I do is I look at the patterns and say, 'Okay, if it starts here, where would I expect the fire to spread?' And that's how I was able to eliminate the living room first, because if the living room was the room of origin, almost all the energy, given that cathedral ceiling, would have gone up to the second floor and nobody would have been able to be on the balcony." John explained how the fire had to start in the den before it found its way upstairs. "When you look at the furnishings there, particularly the wall coverings, the thin wood paneling is the driving force."

"I remember it was regular paneling, thin sheets, 3/16" thick." Leslie knew this because she's a handywoman who could install paneling. "I remember Dad nailed it all up and he used the plastic trim between the panels to make it professional looking."

"It was blue," Lisa added. "But was it pressboard or real wood?"

"It really doesn't matter," John said. "It all burns really quickly, because it is a vertical surface. There's always an airspace behind it, and once the first panel starts to warp, the fire gets behind it. Now you've got a thin material burning on both sides, and it burns really fast." John turned to me. "I was just telling them that the time of flashover, in a living room or a den about the size of yours, is only about ten to twelve minutes from an open-flame ignition. If you have combustible wall coverings, they cut that time in half. Within a few minutes of the first flame hitting that paneling, it is almost unstoppable. That's why so much damage accumulates so quickly in a post-flashover room fire."

My head started to spin, and I wondered whether someone turned up the music, as the sounds of Adele singing "I Set Fire to the Rain" mixed with John's words floated around my head. I gazed around the table at my sisters, who were listening intently.

They talked about the television for a few minutes, about instant-on features. John explained how American TV manufacturers, trying to keep up with the Japanese who were inventing solid-state units, kept the power flowing constantly so that the tubes inside didn't need time to warm up.

"But those components weren't designed to be on continuously; and when they failed, typically three to four hours after being turned off, typically in the middle of the night, people would be asleep in the bedrooms. Fire would start in the living rooms and trap them. There were a lot of fatalities."

"What do you say we can order and then we can keep going?" I asked. This was a lot of information he was giving us, and I didn't want my sisters processing it on empty stomachs.

Menus were passed around, and the conversation shifted.

"They have lunch specials," I observed, looking over the menu. "Do you have a recommendation, John?"

"No, I've only come here for dinners, and it's always been good."

"Garlic prawns," announced Liz.

"Pot stickers are always a good bet."

"What about today's lunch special?"

"As opposed to tomorrow's…"

"That would take a little longer." The welcomed laughter helped break the tension, and we all gave our orders to the Chinese woman waiting patiently to record our choices.

Lisa noticed the book I brought with me. "Is that John's book? Are you going to ask him to sign it?"

"I am, but he doesn't know it yet!" I smiled.

"Always bring a Sharpie when you want an autograph," Lisa advised.

The conversation turned back to the subject at hand. "Can you tell us what are the methods used to determine fire origins now, as opposed to fires then?" I asked. "Because they looked at patterns on the floor and pronounced them to be pour patterns. When they looked at drips upstairs, they said that was evidence of accelerant being splashed over doorways."

"Well, you wouldn't trail flammable liquid into a room you were occupying," John observed, "knowing that that was your way out."

"Yes, that always seemed crazy," I agreed.

"Keep in mind that I've been involved in this field for over forty-two years, and so I was trained the way these investigators were in the original investigation," John began.

"Would you have come to the same conclusion then that they did?" Lisa wanted to know.

"Probably."

"What happened to change your beliefs?"

"Well, I started setting fires." John arranged his napkin neatly on his lap. "Even though I worked for the state crime lab, I was also connected with the California State Fire Marshal arson and bomb unit. Right from the start, we believed if you're going to do training for fire investigators, use live fires. Before that, they would burn a room or a car. Then they'd bring the investigators in and ask what they thought happened. Well, that's not burning anything. That's just repeating the same mistakes over and over again. So we burned somewhere on the order of three hundred or four hundred structures across Northern California from about 1974 to somewhere in the 1980s. We'd create a living room or a bedroom or a garage, and then we'd set fire to it. We watched the dynamics of the fire, observed the time frames, and checked to see where the patterns and the damage were. We realized a lot of what was in the books at the time wasn't right. It didn't match the observations we were making. At first we thought, *Maybe there's something wrong with our tests.* But after the fourth or fifth time of seeing these different time frames and different damage patterns, we realized the books were full of nonsense and we had the right answers."

"Is that when you first wrote the textbook?" Leslie asked.

"The original *Kirk's Fire Investigation* was written in 1969," John began, "and it was the first book on fire investigations written by a scientist rather than a police investigator or firefighter or insurance investigator. Kirk was the professor of criminalistics at UC Berkeley. He did a lot of fire cases and explosion cases, but his work was largely dismissed by the investigative community as just some white-coated academic from the left coast, so they could ignore him. After he died in 1970, his book stayed in print through 1981, when I was approached by the publisher and asked to rewrite it."

It was easy to see how much John was enjoying this. And why not? A free lunch, seated at a table surrounded by enrapt women, expounding on his favorite subject.

"But how do you *set* an accidental fire?" Lisa asked.

"You duplicate the conditions and see what works and what doesn't. Cigarettes are very popular; and finding something that can reliably transition from a smoldering fire, started by a cigarette, to an open flame in a predictable period of time turned out to be quite a challenge, because a cigarette on upholstered furniture can take anywhere from twenty-two minutes to four hours to transition."

"Do you mean that it can really smolder for more than three hours?"

"In some cases, the test materials would smolder for four to six hours. We'd come back, and there'd be a pile of ashes; and we'd say, 'Well, so much for that.'"

John went on to explain how, years ago, at the National Institute of Standards and Technology (NIST), they studied cigarette fires on upholstered furniture, by making mock-ups of chairs, stored under the same conditions and lighted with a cigarette. They used six chairs—two ignited at twenty-two to thirty minutes, two smoldered between an hour and two hours, and the other two never transitioned to flame at all, in the same environment. They drew the conclusion it isn't predictable as to when or whether a fire will start.

Our lunches arrived.

"Garlic shrimp? Chicken? General Pao chicken with fried rice?"

"Does anyone want chopsticks?"

A baby cried a few tables away as we began eating. Throughout the meal, John regaled us with stories of cases he worked on, committees he was associated with, and theories of fire origins that he learned to dispute. Leslie mentioned that she had seen a case on *Forensic Files* that started her thinking differently about arson fires.

"They showcased a fire in an apartment, in the seventies, built the same way ours was, with hardwood floors. The son was accused of murdering his parents, because there were indications of striations on the floors. It turned out that when they were installing the floors, the contractors were thinning the finishes with gasoline. That's why they found flammables on the floor of the apartment. It wasn't anybody; it was in the manufacturing. There wasn't anybody pouring accelerant."

"That was one of my cases," revealed John.

Figures. John knew about every fire we mentioned. There were a number of cases where investigators believed arson was involved. The indications that they believed pointed to arson, such as deeper areas of burned floor, very hot fast fires, and burned carpets, were the result of flashover, not criminal actions.

Trying to steer the conversation back to our fire, I announced, "John made the observation when he was going over our file that it was actually well investigated, which I thought was interesting, because I don't think we felt that at the time."

"Except for the lack of photographs," replied John. "When you read the investigator's narrative, he actually went through every room and identified all the fuel loads. Then he interviewed all of you and asked, 'What do you remember in this room? Imagine you're coming in the door, and what's on your right? What's next?' And that was really important. They all did match."

"That's because we lived in the same house," Liz remarked dryly.

"Our memories worked, in those days," I added.

"Yeah, try that now!" Liz chirped.

John agreed. "You could ask me about my house, and I" go, 'Uh, I don't know.'"

"We had young memories," I nodded. "And this was Detective Buzby who was doing the arson investigations, right?"

"Right, I think that was him. But the way they processed the scene, unfortunately they didn't decide anything until they dug it all out and removed the debris. What we've learned is you document the way the firefighters left the fire and *then* you clean it out and look at patterns and stuff like that. At the time, the dominant theory, which you've experienced, was 'It's what's on the floor that counts. The patterns on the floor tell us everything we need to know.'"

Silverware scraped on plates. I could hear someone in the kitchen chopping food. Music from the overhead speakers provided a soundtrack for John's explanations. "I caught this early on, because the first three or four years I was involved, I was doing lab analysis. Guys would bring debris in, I'd analyze it, and it'd be negative for ignitable liquids. They'd say, 'It can't be.' I'd say, 'Why not?' They'd say, 'Well, it was the lowest point of burn in the house. Everybody knows fires burn up, and carpets can't ignite on their own. And the carpets were burnt; therefore, it had to have been ignitable liquids.' I'd go, 'No.' When we did our tests, the first time we created flashover fire in a structure, we saw carpets disappear, in a post-flashover fire. We told them, 'This is what you guys gotta realize.' It has taken forever, and we still get current reports that say 'We know it was ignitable liquids, because there was a hole burned into the wood floor.'" John looked around the table. "Have you ever tried burning a hole in a wood floor with an ignitable liquid? Does it work? No! And I've done it dozens and dozens of times."

"Because the liquid just burns off, right?" Leslie guessed.

"Right! But if you have post-flashover fire, now you've got the radiant heat blasting down on that wood floor with nothing protecting it, and it goes away. I can burn through a wood floor in a quarter of an inch per minute under flashover conditions." He took another bite of his pot stickers.

Lisa spoke up, "Can you define for us exactly what is flashover?"

John put down his fork. "The flashover fire is a compartment fire where every exposed surface in the room is on fire."

"Okay," Lisa said slowly. She thought for a moment and then turned to Leslie. "Did we really have a bookshelf full of books and a fish tank too?"

Leslie nodded. "Yes, in the den."

Lisa looked back at John. "Would that have had any kind of effect, when the fish tank burst?"

John shook his head and smiled. "It would go 'Pouf!' And it would be gone."

"Do you mean it would evaporate because of the intense heat?"

Every head around the table nodded.

The Chinese woman returned, asking if everything was all right. I knew she meant with our orders, but I felt she could have been asking about our conversation with John. As she turned away,

I asked my sisters, "Do you remember that every door and window was open, including the downstairs sliding glass doors?"

Leslie answered first. "Oh, yes, we kept those open at night."

I thought about life in 1974. Lots of people left their doors and windows open. Homes were often left unlocked. I knew a family who had lost their house keys in the 1950s and never bothered to replace them. Liz must have been reading my mind. "There were no worries back then, of people breaking in or anything like that."

Lisa chimed in. "Plus, we lived right near the bay. The salt air would come in, it was cool, and it was lovely." She sounded like Aunt Betsy.

Liz spoke again, "That's what I kept checking when I woke up, because it was so hot. I wondered, *Is the window open?* And that's when I heard Dad."

Lisa agreed. "It was the heat that woke me up."

"The smoke woke me up," I reminded them.

"And Lisa woke me up, or I would not be here!" Leslie exclaimed. Laughter rippled around the table as her comment broke through the pain that still lay under memories of that awful night.

Lisa pushed her plate away and looked intently at John. "My brain goes all over the place. At first I thought if it was started by a cigarette, then there's no way to tell if somebody accidentally dropped a cigarette or intentionally put a cigarette there. Then I thought Mom could've done that; and then I was thinking, well, so could've I..."

"So could've Dad," Leslie interrupted. "However, there's a big unknown there, and that's whether it would ignite and how long would it take."

"It's like he said," Lisa responded, "but Mom wouldn't leave a cigarette and waste a cigarette like that."

"That's true."

That reminded me. "But she did start a fire in Brigantine, when she fell asleep on the couch."

Leslie remembered. "It started a fire, and I think Dad got the garden hose to put it out. Afterward, there was a blanket over it."

"It was a sweater," corrected Lisa. "It burned a hole about this big." She opened her arms into a circle. "The sweater was covering the hole. We cleaned up that day, and nobody moved the sweater. Nobody. I was a minimalist cleaner, you know. If you didn't tell me directly 'Clean that,' I wouldn't have, so I don't know what you all did. That sweater covered the hole on that sofa for days. I think I remember discovering that giant fire hole when we got new furniture?"

Leslie nodded. "I don't remember when we discovered it, but I don't remember Mom being around after that."

I thought maybe that happened just before one of Mom's many hospitalizations.

We all verified that, during the Ventnor police interviews, we were asked about the Brigantine couch fire, but none of us could understand how they knew about that hole. If no one had called the fire department, how could it have been on record?

Lisa offered a solution. "In a class once, we were talking about fires. Somebody asked, 'What if you start a fire in the kitchen and you're pretty sure you can get it out, but you're not sure?' The teacher said, 'In that case I'd call the fire department, and I'd say, "Hold on. I'm really trying to get this out, but if I can't get it out…"'"

She trailed off as we all laughed out loud at the idea of putting the local fire department on standby.

"That guy was dreaming," chuckled John.

Liz cracked, "Hello, fire department? I might have a fire situation. It's my sister's birthday."

"We're on the way! On the way!" John mimicked.

We talked for a while longer about how the Ventnor police had the Brigantine information. Liz wondered if Mom had told someone while she was hospitalized. Leslie and I wondered if it had been on the insurance application. My father secured fire insurance just months prior when a neighbor's laundry basket which had been next to their furnace ignited and caused a small apartment fire. No one was hurt then, but the incident spurred my father into action.

Someone brought up the television again.

"We had that set in Brigantine," Lisa remembered. "I used to put my feet in that little triangle. It was a triangular panel that pulled out with the controls on it. When it pushed in, it was flat. I used to play with it. I used to lie under it and just push it back and forth with my toes."

John smiled. "See? You loosened the connections. It's all your fault."

Liz pronounced, "It was Lisa! All right, we're done."

Again the laughter broke the tension. I never realized how funny Liz could be.

John looked around the table. "With a public sector investigator, in most jurisdictions, their only job is to check for arson. Their job is not to examine accidental causes. When I talked to DeFebbo, I reminded him about the issue of the television. He said he never thought of it. What they didn't appreciate is what the contribution of the wall paneling would be. We didn't even use the term 'flashover' until the late 1980s. The fire scientists knew about it, but fire investigators did not. One of my early roles, and it still exists to some extent, is bridging between the science and engineering aspects and the scene investigation and investigators, because very few of them know about the science. One of the red flags they would look for was extensive floor damage, because everybody knows fire burns up and out, and therefore the lowest part of the room that's burned has to be the origin. And everybody knows when you drop a match on a carpet, it's not going to burn. Therefore, it has to have help."

"This sounds kind of like voodoo, doesn't it?" someone asked.

John nodded. "People have used that term to describe early fire investigation. One of my major critics used it to describe my application of science as 'twenty-first-century voodoo.' Oh, I'm sorry—'black magic.'"

The Chinese woman returned to clear our plates. John hadn't finished his lunch. "You want to take the pot stickers?"

"Sure. I was talking too much and didn't get a chance to finish them."

"We've hijacked your lunch I'm afraid," I told him. But I could tell that fire investigations were this man's passion, and every man will forego a meal for his heart's desire.

John protested lightly, "But we haven't even gotten to the slides and videos yet!"

The plates were removed to make room on the table to spread out the documents from John's files, the files I had sent to him, as well as the photographs he received from DeFebbo.

John wanted to share the fire dynamics analysis he did on the house. He rifled through the file and pulled out the floor plan of the town house.

"I had to test another hypothesis, and that was the possibility that your father's wood refinishing project involved self-heating finishes, cause those have been a problem for decades." He went on about volatile organic compounds, traditional varnishes, paints that had a solvent, and also what the Egyptians knew five thousand years ago that if you had linseed oil and you spread it on the surface and allowed to react with the oxygen in the air, it would polymerize and form a really nice, waterproof, very permanent varnish.

This time, a Chinese man appeared and asked if we needed anything else. I asked if it was okay that we stayed a while. He nodded his head in agreement and then wandered off to the next table.

"We'll start downstairs," John began, clearing his throat. He pointed to the floor plan. "Here is the living room. Here's the den. The dining room and kitchen had minimal damage, some smoke, some heat because of the open doorways." He moved a bottle of soy sauce out of the way so we could all see the paper in front of him. "All the testimony, including the investigators', said that the stuff used in the refinishing was in the utility room. I thought, *Oooh, it's going to be warm because the water heater's in there, and it could be a point of ignition*, but there's actually a fire-rated door in that doorway. The investigator looked at both sides of the door and said, 'Nope, the inside's still intact. The outside took the beating, but the door was closed, and it didn't start there.' That was good enough for me. Remember when the fire crews arrived, they saw flames coming out the sliders, they made entry through the front door, and they encountered fire here in the foyer." He indicated the front hallway in the floor plan. "They started pushing it back in with the firehoses this way," his finger traced down the hallway toward the den, "which is what they had to do, because there was no other way they could attack. They had to go where they knew the fire would be. I saw minimum damage to the dining room and kitchen, so I'm going to eliminate those. There was minimum damage to the laundry room. I'm going to ignore that. Excluding the utility room, what else do I have?" We hung on every word, waiting for him to answer his own question. "I've got the living room and the den. If I start a fire in the living room, all the hot gases it produces are going to go straight up to the ceiling, and it's going to fill the balcony. Now, I've got furnishings, but I've got painted gypsum walls. So that's going to produce a contents fire more than anything else. If I start a fire in the den, I've got a sofa, I've got bookshelves, I've got this wood paneling on all the walls..."

"All that gorgeous kindling," one of us mused.

John continued. "If I start a fire anywhere in that room, all that paneling is going to ignite. I'm going to drive that room to flashover. Fire's gonna go out into the hall, it's going to cause the sliders to fail, and it's going to come out the sliders; and, as Liz reported, your dad saw the fire coming up from the patio doors. The fire gets into the hallway. You've got a path of floor damage, judging from the descriptions, extending down the hallway."

I noticed in the articles and in interviews with fire investigators, they gave fire a life of its own. Fire had volition, intent, and power; and these men had respect for that.

"One thing we learned about the dynamics of fires is they're going to follow the lines of least resistance. You don't think of it because it's a fluid or it's air, but it does encounter resistance along the walls, so the most intense part of a fire is going to go down the middle of anything—down the middle of a corridor, up the middle of stairs. And what's happening too is that in any confined space, the heat from the walls is going to reflect off the walls and hit the floor." He paused for a moment and made sure we were all with him as he continued with his findings. "In a hallway, the fire is going to create much less damage around the walls, which allows the composite of all the reflected heat be focused where? In the middle of the hallway. You know when you walk down a hallway or up a flight of stairs, do you walk along the wall? No, because you're going to be rubbing against the wall. You're going to walk where there's the least resistance. You're going to walk along the middle of the hallway. Well, fire's going to do the same thing. So we've got a fire pattern coming out of here into the living room, igniting the furnishings in the living room, and that produces a huge amount of heat. We rate fires in terms of their wattage. A candle flame is a fifty-watt fire; a wastebasket is a hundred-kilowatt fire. A living room like this, with noncombustible walls, is going to be maybe a megawatt, maybe two megawatts. It may not even go to flashover, especially with the high ceiling. The den, if you could get enough air in, could support a ten-million-watt fire."

"Why so much more?"

"Because of all that wood, and it's all exposed surface. Fires burn on the surface of any available solid fuel. It's as though you painted the walls with gasoline. It's all going to go, in the space of ten minutes. In ten minutes, that fire would've burned itself out. So you say, 'What happens here?'" John pointed to the living room. "It's going to spill over the balcony, it's going to funnel under the balcony, and you're going to get the kind of damage that you saw in the furnishings under the balcony. It's going to spill out and go up, and I think it was you," pointing to Liz, "who came out on the balcony, but there's all this heat and smoke you couldn't get to the bathroom. You couldn't get anywhere."

Leslie spoke up, "That's when she got burned."

John nodded, continuing. "When we look at the second floor, where's the fire coming from? It's coming up the stairs, so it would've blocked the escape for your parents. It would've extended in, because once this window fails, then it's gonna say, 'Ooh, I got a low-resistance path'; and there was a burn pattern that went right up to the door."

There he goes, I thought, *making the fire talk again.*

"It's possible that somebody made an attempt to open the door in your parents' room and realized there was a big fire out there and they closed the door again. There was lots of smoke. Both parents died essentially of smoke inhalation. But this," he pointed to the stairs, "this is where it's coming up, and now it's spilling down the hallway, and once again it's going to try to get in wherever the windows are open."

Liz interrupted, "I brought it in, because my bathrobe caught fire."

This was news to me. "It did?"

Liz nodded. "First, I walked out. Then I came back in to that first bedroom, because my arm was on fire. I dropped my bathrobe, so that stayed in the bedroom. It was on fire, so that's what caused me to jump."

I must have been at the window myself or outside by then. I marveled at how strong the survival instinct was. My only thought then was to get air in my lungs. It was only after I was outside and breathing fresh air that I thought of the others.

John was talking about the bedroom windows. Once the screens were pushed out, the fire found an easy escape path, and that's why there were burn patterns into both of the bedrooms where we had jumped out the windows. But in Lisa's bedroom, the fire practically stopped at the door, because those windows stayed intact. By knocking out the screens, we made an easier path. That's why the original investigators thought there was accelerant splashed into the rooms. The air from the windows was pulling the fire in.

Liz spoke again, "The newspaper report said that the aluminum ladders the firemen put against the house melted."

John explained that aluminum had a melting point of 1200 degrees Fahrenheit and flame temperatures in a post-flashover fire would range from 1700 to 2000 degrees Fahrenheit. He also told us that the intensity of heat applied to a surface was measured in terms of energy per square meter. If you had a wastebasket fire and you measured the radiant heat flux, just outside the flames that you could see, it's about fifty kilowatts. That would hurt if you put your hand there. If you held your hand further away, it's less intense, so there's less effect. But in a post-flashover fire, the radiant heat flux would range from 150 to 200 kilowatts per square meter.

"That's going to burn through any carpet, any pad, in a matter of a minute or two, especially given today's synthetic materials. Then you have all this beautiful exposed hardwood floor that has a critical radiant heat flux of 20 or 25, and so it's going to ignite. It's going to respond to the same dynamics as the carpet. What we came to realize, in a post-flashover fire, is it's not only a single hot spot. It becomes extremely turbulent. And because of the turbulence of air being sucked in the bottom of a door, it gives you irregular burn patterns. Well, what are these fire investigators trained to look for? Irregular, floor-level patterns, areas of damage not matching the surrounding areas, and that by God meant flammable liquids. Man, that's a tough mythology to overcome."

I thought it was time.

"Les, did you want to look at some of the photos too? Because I know you had some questions."

"Do you have the photos now?" asked Lisa.

"I wanted to see too, John, because I'm not sure how much time you have. And the next steps, did you get the report off to DeFebbo?"

"I sent it the same time I sent you the copies."

I reminded everyone that my goal for our meeting was get closure for all of us and finally get the case closed. Lisa and I started asking questions about it, and DeFebbo said the only reason the case was open was because we opened it. Leslie thought it had always been open, and Lisa explained that it wasn't active before.

"Right," I agreed. "But now it's sitting on someone's desk with a big *open*. What I'd like to do, if everyone has a chance to go through the photos, is figure out what's the process to close it."

"If I didn't put it strongly enough in my report, there's absolutely no evidence of arson here, and everything is entirely consistent with an accidental fire, starting with the den. There's no other feasible, reasonable explanation for which there's any physical evidence," John said, with all the authority of a man who had faced many powerful people and maintained his stance.

I reminded him that I wanted a determination from the Atlantic County Prosecutor's Office, saying that the case was officially closed and ruled as an accident. John emphasized that we could cite his report.

"Is everyone in agreement with that?"

Lisa answered first, "I am!"

John rifled through his oversized black briefcase and pulled out a folder labeled "Photographs, Overton Fire, June 21, 1974." He explained how he compared the photos with the floor plans, lamenting again that most of the pictures were taken after all the debris been removed.

Leslie had a puzzled look on her face. "I thought the whole file was destroyed in the flood?"

"Not all of it."

Liz asked, "How'd that happen? Did the water stop in the middle of the file?"

Lisa and I explained that the flood which destroyed our file was in the county storage, but the Ventnor police had their own files, and that's where these photos originated.

As John spread them out so we could view them, the large eight-by-ten glossy black-and-white photographs seemed to vibrate against the white tablecloth. Even though I had seen them before, I was again shocked by the devastation and amazed still that any of us got out. John walked us through each photograph, explaining his interpretations.

I could again imagine John in front of his class of eager students, explaining again how fire was driven by ventilation and fuel packages, that a post-flashover fire would have flames burning on every surface, and the resulting heat would radiate in all directions, even down. A post-flashover fire might last only a few minutes, burn at an extremely high temperature, and devastate everything in its path. John reiterated that with today's fire forensic science, this case would never have been labeled arson. Mostly likely, it would have been determined to be accidental due to a cigarette left in the couch by Mom.

The first photograph was of the den. Based on the layout of the furniture, it was clear that the fire started there. John illustrated the story of the fire's journey with each succeeding picture. My sisters and I embellished the tale with our memories of the events of that night.

Fueled by the wood paneling, the fire was a blow torch, forcing its way out of the den into the hallway. Under the balcony in the living room, the gypsum wall board failed, and the living room sofa now fueled the fire. A rectangular area on the floor reflected where the synthetic shag rug which used to lie there had sacrificed itself so the fire could continue. The fire burned through the town house, and while still consuming whatever it wanted on the first floor, it advanced up the stairs and shortcut through the balcony. John again and again emphasized there was nothing about our fire to support the claim that a liquid accelerant was poured anywhere or even used.

Photos revealed the cinder blocks between exterior walls, which prevented our fire from visiting the neighbors that night. Viewing the picture of Mom and Dad's bedroom, someone asked how Dad had time to run water in the bathtub. His body was found near their bathroom, while my mother was found on the floor at the end of the bed. John explained that the smoke and the heat, bullying its way in through both their bedroom door and their window over the sliders on the porch, trapped them inside. I remembered the day after the fire, when Aunt Betsy explained to the four of us how they died.

"We think your father was going back to get your mother, but he was overcome by smoke instead."

I thought again what Aunt Millie told Lisa, how my father adored my mother. It was altogether fitting that during his last moments, he was trying to save the love of his life. She was more badly burned and had more smoke inhalation than he did. John surmised that if she had opened the door of their bedroom and a wall of flame met her, she'd take a brunt of both heat and smoke. So she probably shut the door again, retreated, and collapsed at the foot of the bed.

"Keep in mind that death in a fire is normally a combination of three or four different insults," John explained. "As one of my colleagues puts it, if you're forty percent compromised from carbon monoxide, forty percent compromised from heat, and forty percent compromised by cyanide, that's over a hundred percent. You're done. You're going to go, even though any one of those by themselves would not be fatal, to a normal healthy individual. It is a cumulative insult, and your body finally goes, 'I can't do this anymore.'"

No kidding, I thought to myself.

As John gathered the photographs, placed them back in their folder, and stuffed them into his briefcase, there was finally silence around the table. I broke it by telling John our next step was to request the prosecutor's office to close the case.

"Is everyone in agreement with that? Les?"

"It doesn't matter." The way she said this made it sound like it did matter.

"Well, are you still trying to decide?"

"It doesn't matter!"

Lisa said quietly but firmly, "It matters to me."

"Well, then do it!" Leslie angrily retorted.

"Thank you," responded Lisa.

John reminded everyone that DeFebbo agreed with his conclusions.

"That's right," I said, "because you come from a law enforcement and investigative background, which is a good match. We come from the victim's background. That isn't a good match. I was having a difficult time understanding what he was saying, because it was so contrary to forty years of belief that it was an arson fire. And he was trying to rewind my head, and my head wasn't rewinding."

"Right. Well, we've learned a lot in forty years."

"It's a game changer," I told everyone. "For forty years, we thought it was arson, and there was a good chance that Lisa was involved in the arson. Now all that has changed."

"There's absolutely no consistency with an arson determination," John repeated.

"When I met with everyone a couple of years ago, it was a different meeting. In fact, we had never talked about the fire as adults up until then."

"I don't think the four of us ever did," Lisa agreed. "I think we did separately, little conversations among ourselves, but without having any answers. It was just always 'What? What?' and surmisings and shrugged shoulders."

We asked John whether he was keeping the photographs.

"For now, yes. These are the ones that DeFebbo sent me. When we first spoke, he told me he was looking forward to sharing an investigation with me."

"He probably wanted his book autographed too," guessed Lisa.

As he was leaving, John passed out his business card, and Lisa asked him what the Latin *Veritati ex cinerarum* meant.

"Truth out of the ashes."

Finally.

2015

REWRITING HISTORY

Because there's one thing stronger
than magic: sisterhood.
—Robin Benway

Liz, Lisa, Leslie, and Leigh, August 2015

"So what did you think about John?" I asked. I was pretty sure I knew the answer. Lisa obviously liked him. The conclusions he drew from his investigation were favorable to her, so that was a no-brainer. Leslie seemed perturbed about the whole thing. I was willing to bet Liz would go along with whatever the majority decided.

"It sounds like he knows what he's talking about," said Liz.

That was easy.

"Les?"

"Lacking any forensic evidence to the contrary, there's nothing else we can do, really." Her answer felt very controlled. "If that's what you need to do, go ahead and do it." She sat back in her chair and folded her arms across her chest.

"What's that supposed to mean?" demanded Lisa.

"If that's what you guys need to do, go ahead and do it." Her reply was more forceful and brittle. I could feel her words being chipped off, one by one, carefully aimed at each of us.

"You mean close it?"

"Yeah."

"Well, do you have misgivings or something?"

"Lacking any forensic evidence to the contrary, yeah. I don't have anything concrete to hold in my hand. We don't have real files. We've got some pictures; the pictures are good. I was told we didn't have any pictures. Now all of a sudden there are pictures."

I could see that disturbed her.

"They never said they didn't have any photos," I gently explained. "It's just that we couldn't ever get them."

"We couldn't get them. I misunderstood that. I was of the impression the entire file was destroyed."

"The county one was destroyed." I thought we had explained this. "Ventnor had their copy, and the county got their file from Ventnor police."

"Lacking any forensic evidence, if this is what they want to do, it's what we're gonna do." She was sounding like a broken record.

"I don't understand what your question is," prodded Lisa.

"I'm not convinced one way or the other. Because there's no concrete evidence. There are a lot of pictures, and we're never going to get there. Because there are no floor samples in a can, there was no 'This-is-the-point-of-origin-cigarette butt in the couch,' because there's no couch."

I didn't want to present John's case, but I wanted to talk this out again with Leslie. I started walking her back through his report.

"First off, he says all the evidence points to the fire having started in the den."

"Right."

"Because it had all that high heat…"

"Right."

"…It had to have gone straight from there into the living room."

"Right."

"They know now that there is no evidence of these liquid pour patterns. But when I read those in the earlier reports, I thought that's evidence for sure. I mean there's a pour pattern on the floor, and it seemed like they had created this really compelling narrative, right?"

"Right."

"So you are kind of feeling like great and then *this* guy comes and he has another convincing narrative, right?"

"Right, but without any scientific evidence, concrete forensic evidence, that they could test, like the floor…"

"Well, he's saying he *does* have evidence. That's what this book is based on," I indicated his textbook, "all the fires he set and what he learned from them."

"Um-hum." I still heard the hesitation in her voice. "I do understand the new science," she added. "It's actual *science* now, whereas before it was…"

"What do you think about the photos we saw today?"

"Very compelling, interesting." She removed her glasses and began rubbing them with one of the cloth napkins.

"Is this the first time you've seen them?" asked Lisa.

"The first time I saw them, I thought I was going to be sick," I told her. "It's much easier looking at them a second time. What did you feel like, seeing them today?"

There was a quiet moment where Leslie seemed to be gathering her thoughts, like storm clouds forming in her head. She finished rubbing her glasses and put them back on.

"It's just different."

"And we're happy," offered Lisa.

"It wasn't anything I didn't expect. I'd read the report, and I knew about the science because I'd seen it on TV. I read the stories that you sent me over the weekend."

"The problem, I think, and I agree with you Les," I began, "is that this started when we were kids. And now that we're all adults and we're probably a little bit more sophisticated than even some of the people who worked on this case, we're able to review it with adult eyes and adult intelligence."

"Forty years removed," Les said softly. I could sense her calming down.

"All of a sudden it's like 'Really? Really?' You know the way they investigated. John said he felt it was well investigated, but I still felt like the investigation was lacking."

"I don't feel it was well investigated at all." She took a breath. "I think one of the things that bothers me is: What happened forty years ago that shut it down? If they had a finding of arson, why wasn't it ever investigated further?"

Lisa answered, "Don't you remember what they said to us then? Mr. Cole said there were four girls and their parents had died. There's no way to *know* if it was arson. The evidence pointed to the fire having started from the inside and that if it *was* arson, then the only person who could have logically done it was Mom, right? I never understood how anybody could think that I could get ahold of some substance to ignite a fire that nobody would know what it was. I don't understand how anybody could think that."

"It wasn't you," insisted Leslie. "It wasn't that *you* had started the fire; it was that your friends did it for you or your friends did it without your knowledge."

I went back to the evidence, keeping close watch on Leslie's reactions. She had her hands propped under her chin, and she was leaning in to listen as I spoke.

"During the first weeks after the fire, there's a couple of things that happened. Lisa's former principal called in, the only tip that they had. He said she was heard talking to other kids about how to start a fire or asking how to start a fire. He thought that Lisa was a wild kid, so they started looking at her and talking about her friends. That led them more profoundly to the sense that it was arson. I don't think they looked at anybody *but* Lisa." I let this settle in before I went on. "Then Uncle Doug said that he was called in and told by Perskie, Uncle John, and Maurie Cole if they took this any further, no good would come of it, because a young girl's life would be ruined. There are also some other pieces here. One, Lisa and I asked Uncle John, while we were sitting on the deck one morning, about the fire and what he knew. He said he wasn't directly involved. He was busy being a mayor and managing his real estate and insurance company. Uncle John wasn't involved with our estate. Maurie Cole was the one who was running the show. *He* was the one who hired Marvin Perskie. Maurie settled the estate; Maurie set up the Overton Children's trust fund. Maurie was directly involved. When we asked John about the Overton case, he said, 'I didn't know about any of that. Had I known, I would've tried to help.' He also said, rather vehemently, that he never tried to shut down the case. He wouldn't have done that, because that would've been illegal. So that was John Rogge."

I took a deep breath. The couple at the next table finished their meal, and the Chinese man was taking their plates, asking whether they wanted anything else. Lyrics from "Call Me Maybe" drifted into my consciousness from the overhead speaker, *I trade my soul for a wish, Pennies and dimes for a kiss, I wasn't looking for this, But now you're in my way.*

"Then, Marvin Perskie wrote a letter to the prosecutor's office which said, 'My client is not going to talk, nor will she cooperate.' So they had a dead end on that. They had no other information at all, to do anything with this. There was nothing left to investigate. The samples that came back, from the state police, tested negative."

"For accelerants?" Leslie asked.

"Correct. They had no evidence. When Lisa and I talked to Jimmy Barber and Chuck DeFebbo and a couple of other people, they all agreed that without evidence, the authorities couldn't do anything. No one in our family was going to push it anymore. They thought, *Enough has happened to these four girls. Let's just move on.* I think in their heart of hearts, they made the best decision with the information that they had at the time. They didn't have enough to prosecute, really. Maybe they thought they could put Lisa in juvie for a couple years, until she turned eighteen, but without the evidence they didn't have a case. And that's what was hanging this thing up."

"Why wouldn't they look anywhere else?" asked Liz. She had been playing with the silverware that had been left on the table.

"But where would they look?" I answered.

"What about that car, the station wagon that sped off before the fire started?"

"They did look at that. It was a dead end."

"Where did we decide that Mom did it?" demanded Leslie. A hint of anger had crept back into her voice.

"I didn't," Liz said. She started sweeping up fortune cookie crumbs using John's business card.

"I decided that Mom did it," Lisa broke in. "Because I'm the only person who knows it wasn't me. And if it was *some*body…"

"That's why Uncle Doug was very emphatic with me," Leslie realized, "about making sure that I understood that *you* did it, Lisa, because our mother couldn't have done it. It was *you* pushing Mom. Can I have some tea?"

I was so involved in our conversation I hadn't noticed the Chinese woman arrive at our table and ask if there was anything else we'd like.

"When it was told to us that this was an arson fire, we had to find somebody to blame," I explained. "And what we learned was Lisa was the most likely suspect. She was the last one in the house that night, the first one to escape out the window, and the most outwardly angry of all of us. But the possibility that she had done this and kept her mouth shut about it all these years or that any of her little friends had kept their mouths shut doesn't make any sense. Teenagers break like this." I snapped my fingers. "They don't keep a secret. And they were all questioned, carefully. Someone would have said something. Something would have broken if it was those kids, you know?"

"It was the times. They were the worst of times…" Leslie quoted. "Thick as thieves they were…"

Again the laughter punctuated the intensity of our conversation. The sounds of chopsticks and forks scraping plates mixed with the music from the overhead speaker. *Confusion never stops, closing walls and ticking clocks*, sang Coldplay.

"So they interviewed the kids who were out in the parking lot," I continued, "and the cops knew exactly what they did that night.

The only thing that made sense was if it was arson, then it had to be somebody from the family. That's why this has been so muddy. Lisa was treated at the time as a person of interest, but she had Marvin Perskie hired for her so she was off limits. Detective Fields was investigating this. And he already..."

"He had a hard-on for Lisa," Leslie interrupted.

"Right, it was for *all* the teenage kids in Ventnor Heights at the time."

"He was Officer Krupke," Liz put in.

"He thought he was Serpico," Lisa emphasized.

"We called him Serpi-cool," added Les, "and he was going to take everybody down. Hell, I remember him coming to the house, long before the fire. He was just Mr. Cop, and you were the juvenile delinquent, you and your miscreant friends. They were dealing drugs, smoking pot."

Find out what we're made of, you can count on me, sang Bruno Mars above my head.

"Okay," said Les. "But what about the quote about Buzby having 'evidence that's gonna blow this thing wide open'? Wasn't it just grandstanding?"

"No," I said emphatically. "Everybody I talked to said, 'Buzby? He would never have said that. It's not his style.'"

"Then why it is in the report?"

I let everyone know the best reason I could come up with what Jimmy Barber said. The cop who had put that note in the report was known as a blowhard who had a real problem with somebody.

"He was making him look bad, by making a quote from Buzby that sounded bigger and better than it was. Either that or just making a joke," suggested Liz.

"Not so funny," I pronounced.

Lisa spoke next, "Okay, I just want to say this. I have post-traumatic stress disorder (PTSD). We all do, from being a survivor of a tragedy. You might not have the diagnosable condition, but you definitely have some of the symptoms." She turned to Leslie, who had rolled her eyes when Lisa mentioned PTSD. "I can tell you don't believe me. Anyway, it was pointed out to me that not only do I have

PTSD from being a victim of a fire but I also have it from living the drug lifestyle. But I also have it from being an innocent suspect. I know that to you it might not be apparent and that to you it may be something to be taken lightly, but it has profoundly affected me my entire life. The way that I operate in my life, how I interact with people, is because of this cloud. So this outcome is just miraculous to me. Finally." She took a breath and continued. "But the fact that Aunt Jill died, because she was one of the people who blamed me, she died thinking I was an arsonist and a murderer. It really hurts. And I miss what Liz had with Aunt Jill."

"I don't think she really associated you with being an arsonist and a murderer," Liz consoled her. "She associated you with the horrible person who got in a fight with her in the kitchen, when you were both on the floor wrestling around. That was the Lisa that she didn't like."

"Right," added Leslie, "that she didn't like and would not forgive."

"You have to remember at that time Aunt Jill was also a drinker. I'd get up in the morning, and I'd go to the cabinet that was above the stove. I'd grab my box of cereal. Aunt Jill would reach up in the cabinet next to it and grab the bottle of booze and pour it into her coffee. Then she'd go and get dressed for work," Liz remembered.

Les agreed. "She didn't have a hangover in the morning; she was drinking in the morning."

"But she wasn't a falling-down drunk, and she wasn't a mean drunk," Liz went on.

"Mom couldn't function, but Aunt Jill did," Leslie noted.

"But Mom was drugged," Lisa protested.

"Maybe she just made bad decisions, like saying really mean things to Lisa," I tried to defend Jill.

"Oh, yes," Liz agreed. "She was an instigator, like Lisa was. The two of them were probably two peas in a pod if you ever thought about it, except that Aunt Jill was the adult and should've known better. She would push Lisa's buttons. She would push anybody's buttons, till the day she died."

"She's still pushing buttons from beyond," Leslie added. "She was a tough cookie, and she was a stickler for the worst minutiae."

"I always tell people that I don't have any tact whatsoever, because of the fact that my aunt didn't teach me any!" Liz laughed. "'Get your elbows off the table,' that's all she'd say. She couldn't say, 'Would you please remove your elbows from the table?' She taught me that you said *what*ever you wanted to say, you said it to *whom*ever you wanted to say it to, and you said it *when*ever you wanted to say it. But Lisa would react!"

Leslie agreed. "Lisa was *so* angry, so angry at that age. Angry, mean, and horrible at that age. And then having an arson cloud over your head sure didn't help matters…"

I reminded them of the custody thing.

"That's right," Liz nodded. "I remember Uncle Doug sitting us down and saying, 'Well, nobody else wanted you, so I got you. Now you're going to deal with it.'"

I added, the situation that you all went into after the fire was challenging for everyone.

It was Liz who brought the conversation back to the question at hand.

"By having the case closed," she turned to Lisa and me, "I can understand your reasons for wanting it closed, and I can understand Leslie's reasoning wanting it open. I kinda say, 'What the hell. Leave it open.' Because if they find the guy walking down the street who threw the Molotov cocktail into the house and we need him convicted of murder, you know we need to leave it open. But that's not gonna happen. There's no evidence of that. I understand that. I'm the one who, all my life, believed it was the faulty wiring behind the couch. Now, it wasn't the couch; it was the TV. I can deal with that. I never thought it was Lisa. I never thought it was Mom. I never thought it was Dad. I never thought it was Leigh, me, Leslie, or the guy walking down the street with the station wagon."

"Right," laughed Lisa. "Anyone caught walking down the street with a station wagon at that hour of the night deserves punishment."

Liz smiled and shrugged and continued speaking, "I would say leave it open because it doesn't bother me, but I can understand you guys wanting it closed. So I don't care, you know. Close it."

"Close it," said Leslie. The tone of her voice was not defeat, but acquiescence.

"Close it," Liz repeated.

"Close it. Put it closed. Make it closed. Just, enough is enough," Leslie fired off. "I mean the science is good. You've got good science. Go with it."

Lisa asked if the report still had to be kept private. I explained I had wanted the four of us to meet and discuss the findings before anyone shared it with others. Now that we had talked it over, it was public as far as I was concerned, except I didn't want to find it showing up on Facebook.

Lisa said she only wanted to tell Aunt Betsy about it, maybe even tell Uncle Doug too. I let her know I did talk to Uncle Doug, and to Kim.

"Uncle Doug called me last week," Lisa announced.

"I heard about that," Leslie remarked. "It was a miracle, after forty years."

"Was it hard to talk to him? After all those years?" I wanted to know. "Because I would be bitter. I would be extremely bitter. You don't seem to be. That's the miracle I see. I would have so much anger to deal with. He was supposed to be your parent, for God's sake. He was supposed to have taken you in."

"I was angry for a very long time. I still have anger," Lisa told us. "But I know that anytime that I feel anger, it's because I'm hurt. Anger is a secondary emotion. I know that, but I'm not going to go to my grave hating and bittering. I'm not. I'm going to let go. If I hate somebody or if I'm bitter and angry, it's not hurting them; it's hurting me. I spent a lot of my life hurting myself and the people around me, until I learned I didn't have to do that. I realized we are all human and we make mistakes. Once I was able to forgive the people who hurt me, I was able to stop hurting myself."

"Well, my regret is that we didn't investigate this sooner," I said. "I wasn't in a place to do it sooner…"

"Nobody was," Lisa pointed out.

"I think what's interesting, though, is you and I have been adversarial from the time you were born, because…"

"You're not the boss of me!" Lisa quoted. That was her response to anything I asked her to do, back when we were kids.

"Les taught me to walk and talk, and Liz was the baby. So you and I have had the most tumultuous relationship of the sisters."

"It was competition for Mom's attention. That's what it was," Leslie offered.

"I'm just so happy for me to get closure," I told them. "I'm happy for me that it's accidental because that whole taint of arson has made me fearful and second-class damaged. I don't feel damaged anymore. I feel bad. I feel sad. I feel terrible. But I don't feel so damaged."

"I'm just upset I'm not going to get any more mileage out of it," Leslie lamented. "But maybe the irony of it just adds to it. Isn't it crazy, after forty years, we finally find out, nope, nobody did it!"

"Before I started this journey," I began, "I had been living under the belief that we had a typical family until this tragedy hit. I guess I blocked from myself a lot of the bad stuff. I remembered that Mom was sick and had to go in the hospital sometimes, but it wasn't until I started digging down and talking that all this other stuff came up. Did you guys have any of the same reactions? I mean how did you feel about our lives?"

"I just remember that it was all fucked up," Leslie reported. "We didn't know that there was love in the family. I was *told* I was loved, but I didn't *feel* loved. That's just the way it was. And it was…"

"It was an assumption," Liz finished.

"We weren't hugged," stated Lisa.

"No hugs, no good night kisses," Leslie reminded us. "I remember when Dad tried patting my hand one time to apologize for hitting me in the mouth all the time with my braces. I finally had to ask Mom, 'Tell Dad to stop smacking me in the teeth and hit me anywhere else. When he keeps hitting me in the mouth, he's cutting the inside of my mouth from my braces. Could he please stop doing it?' I was going up the stairs one day, and Dad came over. I had got my hand on the railing. He reached out so he could apologize to me. I pulled my hand away. I was afraid of being touched."

I didn't remember any of this. And why would it be okay to hit a child on *any* part of their body? It was not how I raised my children.

"You were the golden child," Les reminded me. "You never did anything wrong."

"I did with Mom," I said. "Mom and I battled it out. But I was a co-conspirator with Dad. When Dad went to work, he needed me to take care of you guys. He showed me how to tape the door to see if Mom was going out to cheat on him. He left me at home to kind of keep an eye on Mom. I had to hide the alcohol."

"We all had to do that," Les and Liz said at the same time.

"He hit me," declared Lisa. "He backhanded me out of the chair one time at the dinner table. And you, Leigh, we called you 'Miss Antiseptic.'"

"A place for everything and everything was always in its damn place," Les quoted.

"You used the damn white gloves to check the windowsills when I cleaned the bedroom!" exclaimed Liz.

"But that was my reaction to chaos!" I defended myself.

"Exactly," agreed Leslie. "Exactly. My reaction was to make sure that everything was fixed, that everyone had their shoes, the bows were tied, the zippers were zipped…"

"Because we know I couldn't do that!" I reminded them.

"Right," stated Leslie. "Everything had to be perfect. Everything that Leigh couldn't do, I did."

"I read books," Lisa put in. "I hid from all of it that way."

"And I created chaos," Liz said so softly I almost didn't hear her.

We all sat quietly for a moment, each lost in the memories of our childhood before the tragedy. I puzzled over the idea that Liz could possibly have been the one to create chaos, when it was Mom who caused all the chaos. A baby fussed at the next table, and I heard the mother talking softly to calm the child down. I flashed back to the DNA report.

"Do you guys think Dad knew I wasn't his kid?"

"Yeah," Liz surprised me with that answer.

"Remember what Aunt Millie said?" Lisa asked. "She had a really high opinion of Dad and a pretty low opinion of Mom. I asked her whether she knew anything about your parentage. She said, this is paraphrasing, that *she* was a good Christian girl and Mom would not have confided her bad behavior to her. But she said Dad was a great man, a wonderful man. She asked him, once, 'With all the things that Nancy does, why do you put up with her?' And his response was 'Oh, that's easy, because I love her.'"

That didn't answer my question, so I asked again.

"But do you think he knew?"

"I don't know. He was a smart man. I'm sure he could've figured it out."

"But something that I have wrestled with is Jill and Doug; *they* knew."

"I think that rots," said Les. "It could be that the story that Mom just met somebody in a bar down in Atlantic City was correct."

"Why didn't they know who?" wondered Lisa.

"Doug told me that he did not remember," I told them. "He told me that some place, some bar, or something. His story kept changing. I did ask again when I was back there for Aunt Jill's funeral. He was on pain meds, but he just wouldn't tell me anything. I say they were cowardly, because we were coming from that diagnosis with Drew."

Les shook her head. "That's the part that really is unconscionable."

"I tried to give Jill and Doug the benefit of the doubt. They were loyal to Mom, but their loyalty didn't run to me. That made them loyal to Dad. And Doug made some comment to Kim, saying 'We don't want her to go out and start looking for her father.'"

"But that makes you really want to look," Liz pointed out.

"And it added a new twist to this whole fire thing," I agreed. "I mean it goes from arson to accidental. It goes from being a sibling to a half-sibling. There are more surprises in this story than a Hitchcock movie."

"Right," agreed Les. "Every assumption we started with has been blown out the window."

The couple with the baby had finished their meal, gathered their belongings, and were headed for the exit. I looked around and noticed we were the only lunch customers still in the restaurant. A young Chinese man, probably a family member of the owners, was dragging a vacuum out from behind a trifold Shoji screen. In the corner, an older woman was shelling peas into a large bucket.

"We trusted those people, those adults, back in the day; and maybe they did protect us," I said. "I don't know if they did protect us, it was at Lisa's expense. Lisa was having all those other issues, so there was no champion for her at that point. Frankly, there was no champion for any of us, even Betsy and John, as good as they were. They had their own lives and their own kids. I just kept my head down and kept the house clean. And Betsy said, 'You turned out better than we ever thought.'" That brought laughter. I continued, "Now, Jill and Doug. Well, Jill was in the throes of some major alcoholism then. They had their kids, and Doug was doing this remodel; and apparently, which I believe is true, they knew very little of what was going on in Brigantine. Grandmom had just died…"

"And they were fighting over that," interrupted Lisa.

"We walked in, right in the middle of that," Leslie pointed out.

"What has made it a little strange to me was that for so long Jill and Doug were in lockstep with Mom. And they had just been fighting with her. You know, she was wild. Jill and Mom had not gotten along when they were younger; but as soon as she's dead, all of a sudden, it's like—"

"She's a saint!" Leslie finished the sentence for me.

"That's the way the mind-set is," Liz explained. "You respect your elders, and you respect the dead."

"Right," Les agreed. "The dead can do no wrong."

Lisa shook her head. "That's what we were wrestling over in the kitchen. That's why Aunt Jill and I were fighting. She said to me, 'You're a slut, just like your mother was,' and that was when I lunged at her."

"Now, notice that she called our mother a slut, which obviously meant, I mean, she was probably right about that," I pointed out, and we all laughed at that. It seemed to me that was proof that Jill knew back then that I had a different father.

"Jill didn't like me either," Leslie put in, "because of how much I reminded her of Mom, more than Lisa. And that's why I left a week before my eighteenth birthday. We were too much of a resemblance to Mom; and that's why Jill didn't like us, either one of us, because of how much like Mom we were."

Les and Lisa did look more alike when we were kids, so I understood her point.

"But still," I said, "I applaud Doug and Jill, because I can't imagine me taking on three or four kids in a situation like that. It was just a lot, especially when you worked full-time. And all that family stuff that was going on…"

The Chinese waiter was back.

"Water anyone?"

The conversation trailed off while our glasses were refilled. After he finished, I thought it was nearly time to wrap everything up. I had fought traffic on the way to the restaurant, and I didn't want to hit the afternoon rush hour on the way home.

"Do you guys feel like we've really talked it through and come to any kind of—"

"Conclusions?" asked Leslie. "No. Acceptance, yeah. Even though I always accepted that it was arson."

"And I always thought it was an accident," Liz stated.

"What about you, Lisa? What did you think it was? What did you tell people about it?"

We all turned to Lisa, who took a drink of water before she answered. She held her glass tightly as she spoke, "I'd say that people thought I was a person of interest or the suspicion fell on me, but I *did* think it was arson because that's what they told us and that's what people were holding on to. And I understand what you were saying about my friends, but I didn't have that kind of friends. I can't imagine asking somebody, 'Hey, you want to set a fire for me?' 'Ahh, yeah, sure, what time?' You know? I didn't have that kind of friends." She put the glass back on the table.

"I know why I held on to arson," Leslie told us. "Because arson would have meant that there was a reason for the fire, whereas an accidental fire had no purpose, no reason. It was just an accident; it was just a thing that happened."

"That's right," I agreed. "Arson has intent."

"It has answers," Lisa reminded us. "I mean it has more questions, but…"

"…There's a reason," continued Les. "It means it's intentional, that it was meant to have occurred. Somebody was a catalyst to creating an event, whereas if it was just a random event, accidental…"

"…Then you had to bring God into the picture!" Liz finished. She laughed heartily, and we all joined in, because Leslie didn't believe in God. The rest of us did, and we often teased Leslie about it.

"No, we didn't," Leslie retorted.

I didn't want to get into that discussion again. "I say, 'Shit happens.'" No one laughed.

"Whereas if it's arson," Leslie continued. "It's too horrible to have imagined that there was no reason, that it was just a completely random occurrence in the universe, and I think arson just gave it a reason."

"Maybe it was a random act, an act of kindness," Liz offered.

There was silence while everyone mulled that over. Leslie spoke first, "A random act of kindness. Yeah, that works. Because I always did think of it as an act of kindness. I absolutely did."

"I think we all did, eventually, because it gave us the ability to get out of a really bad situation," I summed it up. "Someone made a comment about the Overtons nearly imploding upon themselves. I find sometimes, when life gets to be so completely out of whack, just when you get to a point where you can't stand it, something changes. I remember just when I thought things couldn't get any worse with Drew, he died. And that was actually a blessing, because his muscular dystrophy was so progressive. So it seemed like when things couldn't possibly have gotten any more dysfunctional, this house—"

"Right, it imploded on itself," Les interjected.

"And now we're free. I thought someone had said we're free, free at last."

"I said it," Lisa admitted. "And so did Martin Luther King, but he said it first."

I thought about what Liz said at our last meeting. It seemed that, because of the tragedy, our lives had turned out better.

"We all got to go to college," Lisa reminded us.

"Right," Leslie added. "Remember Dad always said that he was giving us fifty bucks and a ladder, to get out of the house, to get married."

"You mean for the elopement," Lisa said. "Because we had second-story bedrooms."

"And the joke was I would get the stepladder because I was on the first floor in Brigantine," I remembered. "Because we grew up with 'there's no money.' There was never any money—"

"And there wasn't gonna be money," put in Liz.

"Food was starting to become a luxury, which was why we all scattered or got jobs or stayed at friends' houses. It was tough."

"Right. If you wanted anything, by the time we were teenagers, you had to get it yourself," Leslie remembered. "In those days, my available cash went for drugs and cigarettes."

I could see how our family's lack of money could have led to a sense of desperation, and I wondered about the anger. Both Leslie and Lisa had it, more than anybody. I thought of something else.

"Do you think there's a direct correlation between the lack of money and Dad hitting you guys all the time? Because it's known that children who are hit a lot or who are disrespected end up with anger issues."

Lisa answered, "Probably, but I don't think that was the main thing. You could say it is a correlation more than a direct relation. However, to me, it was more the sense that what I was being told and what's expected of me and all the rules and everything were frickin bullshit. You know what I mean? It was like you could only eat carrots, but then if you ate carrots, you got in trouble. You couldn't go do this. It was just the inconsistency of everything. It was just the lies of everything. It was that 'You gotta pretend everything's okay,' when everything's *not* okay. It was 'Just pretend nothing bad's happening.' Your mom's in a psychiatric institution, but just go ahead and go to school. It was like 'What the hell?'"

Leslie agreed. "Pretend everything's normal and smile."

"Right."

"And be happy."

"Well, *that* pissed me off. It was the hypocrisy of it all that pissed me off. I don't know if I saw it and felt it more than others. I don't know. That's one of the things Uncle Doug said, that maybe I was more sensitive. But I know that it pissed me off. And I know that not having a voice pissed me off. And I know that there's my mom, falling down drunk, wasted, whatever, and incapable of being a mother and demanding respect because she's my mother. I'm like 'Get the hell out of here, lady. Respect is earned, and you haven't earned mine.' I was angry about that. I did not like being powerless. It created anger in me. I don't know why I react with defiance and anger, but I do. It's as if you were to tell me 'This is blue.'" Lisa pointed to the white table-cloth. "No, it's not blue, and I would argue with you about it, at that time. In those days, I would've pulverized. I would've argued you into hell. Now I'd say, 'Oh well, you have the right to be wrong.'"

The four of us laughed at this. I noticed Leslie and Liz checking their phones.

"Traffic's cool so far," Liz announced. We each had a few-hour drive ahead of us, and the Bay Area traffic was notorious for getting snarled during commute hours.

"I was thinking of that too."

I cleared my throat and looked around the table at my sisters. "I think our thoughts and feelings as adults have become more important now, especially because of what I have been reading about these convictions being overturned. Our story is part of a larger story, because it seems like we got caught up in something that happens to a lot of people."

"In that sense, we're lucky," Lisa noted.

"We dodged a bullet on that," Liz added. "Can you imagine if we had to welcome Lisa home from prison?"

Leslie laughed. "We'd all say, 'I ain't taking care of her!'"

We laughed, but the four of us knew that somehow, we had been saved from a fate worse than the one we survived. We had the feelings people had when they missed their flight and later learned their plane crashed, full of joy and relief that we were not on that plane, but full of sorrow for the others who had flown their final journey without even knowing it.

EPILOGUE

Turn your wounds into wisdom.

—Oprah Winfrey

Family reunion, August 2015

My life has been defined by the fire. Many cultures have rite-of-passage ceremonies, which celebrate a person's crossover from childhood into adulthood. But my transition out of youth was marked by a tragedy that killed my parents and separated me from my sisters and our home. The fire took away any chance of our family recovering from its dysfunction or Mom ever getting well. It stole the opportunity for Dad to walk me down the aisle and give me away when I got married or for Mom to be a grandmom, hopefully better than she was at being a mom. The fire robbed us of the chance to grow up in the family where we originated. When Mom and Dad died, we really were on our own. By age seventeen, I had developed many of the adult coping skills and determination that I needed to succeed. What I lacked, Betsy and John Rogge helped to fill in those voids. I am not sure my sisters had these benefits. As the oldest, I had more of the good years, the early years, when Mom was still surrounded by the people who supported her throughout her life.

But I also developed a need to separate from my family to protect myself. Mom's mental illness, alcoholism, and poor health disrupted the foundation on which we built our childhood. Her suicide attempts spilled into our teenage years and became a catalyst for rebellious behavior by two of my younger sisters. Dad's lack of control over his family and finances, which were slipping away on the brink of personal bankruptcy, made an already bad situation worse. The times in which we grew up, the 1960s and 1970s, further conspired to shape the family dysfunction by treating mental illness with powerful, narcotic medications, which in Mom's case changed an emotionally distraught individual into a suicidal psychotic. The shame and stigma caused our family to adopt the military's stance of "Don't ask. Don't tell."

My journey to find the truth has been a long and arduous road with unexpected consequences. The path was littered with police and fire reports, autopsies and evidence, news clippings, and old family letters. My belief that my sister Lisa was in some way involved in the deaths of our parents had calcified over the years and became a part of me. But finally, learning the truth that the fire was accidental, not arson, leached away my old beliefs. Early on, I wondered what would happen if Lisa *was* guilty and charged, since there is no statute of limitations for murder. What if she was proven guilty in a court of law? What would that do to our family? Who would raise her two daughters? I struggled with this for months, wondering whether I was doing the right thing. Could the truth destroy our family more than the fire had? Betsy Rogge counseled me not to dig the matter up; she insisted that what was done was done. But I wanted the truth. In spite of my fears, I needed to take the plunge into the past. I would deal with consequences later.

During the course of my investigation, I reached a place where I became able to forgive my past and the ghosts that haunted it. Somehow, I gained a bigger heart to forgive my mom for who she was. I found compassion for her mental illness which was never properly treated and understanding for my dad who enabled her. With this new heart, I realized that I also had found the willingness, the love, and the courage to forgive whoever set our house ablaze. Even if it did turn out that Lisa had done it, I would be able to forgive her too.

But as it turned out, there was no villain. No one was charged with arson or murder, because we learned our fire was not a crime; it was an accident. Lisa had been telling the truth all along—she was not guilty, not involved in any way. I gained a new sense of compassion for what we went through. I felt sorry for us, we who spent forty years with the burden of not knowing the truth. I am truly sorry it took so long to get the answers we so badly needed. Lisa was finally vindicated, and eventually, my doubts were erased. After consideration of the reports and conclusions of John DeHaan, the Atlantic County Prosecutor's Office officially closed the Overton fire case on December 1, 2014.

But, as I soon learned, not all families are this fortunate. There are hundreds of cases of persons wrongfully accused of arson and crimes they did not commit. Today, in states like Texas, fire cases are being reopened and reviewed, based on new fire science forensics. And some of those convicted who were innocent, but served years of hard time, are now being released from prison and set free to recapture their lives. I cannot imagine what that must be like, to be accused of starting a fire (that killed your loved ones) when you were an innocent victim—that is the real tragedy. I do not know how someone can move on and start over. It was hard enough for me to survive our fire. At least I had my life to live.

Another truth revealed was an unintended consequence of my research and investigation: my paternity. Although really never in question (except for comments I heard growing up like "You are so different from your sisters"), tests revealed that I truly am different from my sisters. Because my mother cheated on her husband, my "dad" Frank was not my father. I'm only a half-sibling. I have no way of knowing who my "DNA dad" is or whether he is still alive. It is my hope that someone reading this may come forward with new information.

At first, the paternity news hit me with a terrible sense of loss and a feeling of being unmoored and at loose ends. At least from a genetic sense, I can only account for half of myself. This turned out to be problematic when I learned my son, Drew, had Duchenne muscular dystrophy and I was the carrier. (None of my sisters are carriers.) Also, the fact that Doug and Jill knew about this and kept it a secret simply astounds me. One would think they would have shared this material fact with me when I became an adult or at least when I was struggling with my son's illness and later his death. But their code of silence was kept, and the past remained in the past until now.

Now is the time to forgive. Mom and Dad/Frank are dead. Drew is dead. Jill is dead. While I regret that I can only provide my daughter with partial genetic information, this is our reality. As I think about it though, I realize that Frank Overton was my real dad and always will be. I grew up with him for a very short seventeen years. We shared our lives. I wonder if he knew that I was not his firstborn.

I think back to a discussion I had with Betsy Rogge. We brought up the old nature versus nurture debate and what factors affected most a person's personality traits. I always laughed and said I hoped it was environmental, because I wanted to be like John and Betsy who were caring, devoted, successful, and stable. Still today, both in their 90s, they remain a tremendous loving influence on my life.

Lisa has told me how important it was to her that I undertook my investigation. She always knew she was innocent, she said, but she didn't want to be like OJ, out on the golf course, looking for the real killers. The opportunity to write and right this story has been part of my journey and provided me with the perseverance to find the truth. The struggle to remember and find my voice that was silent for so long made me strong, so now I can face my past; I can live fully in the present and embrace the future. My journey brought me back to who I am. It brought me closer to my sisters and our daughters. It exposed the truth and started healing a forty-year-old wound. By writing this story, I exorcised the demons of doubt and fear that plagued our family. I am no longer afraid of my memories.

Today, our journey continues. Leslie is always on the go, and when not working or taking classes at the state or as a notary, she divides her time between her grandchildren and working on her house. Her daughter Leah, whom Leslie says turned out just fine in spite of some of her best efforts to the contrary, juggles a husband, two school-aged children, one German Shepard, three cats, one desert tortoise and a management career at Target.

Leslie inherited Dad's carpentry skills and Mom's creativity. She is the sister we go to if we need something fixed, remodeled, or assembled. She is the family historian with an exquisite ability to remember details of our childhood. Back in 1989, she gathered the recipes from our childhood and typed up a delightful family cook-book, now in its third edition (with another update in the works).

After twenty-one successful years in the finance industry, Liz is a self-employed Certified Notary Signing Specialist. Her passion, though, is all things cooking—especially downsizing family-size rec-ipes to empty nest size. If we have a kitchen question, she has the answer. She visits Uncle Doug at his new assisted living facility in Michigan and is the family event coordinator, the sister who soothes ruffled feathers and provides guidance when asked.

With her oldest daughter a graduate student at San Diego State University, and her youngest transitioning from community college to her junior year at Humboldt State, Lisa has moved with her hus-band to rural Kentucky, where while fixing up the farm, she is work-ing on her memoirs. Lisa has been clean and sober for fourteen years and is active in the local twelve-step fellowship. A published writer, some of her works can be found on Amazon.com.

When I began this book, I never imagined I would learn so much about myself. Although it seemed like I lost my childhood and I am not sure about half my DNA, the insight I've gained and the truths I've accepted have brought healing and wholeness to our family. My sisters and I are bound by time, forgiveness, love, and compassion, which is more important than DNA. Forgiveness is an elixir, a taste of the fountain of youth. The strength to persevere, and the faith to believe, led to the truth. But most importantly, my sisters and I have strengthened our bonds and celebrated our sisterhood. We are survivors, not victims, with the courage to accept the past and live well in the present.

ACKNOWLEDGMENTS

It is a tragedy to survive a house fire and lose loved ones. But it is a far greater tragedy to be falsely accused of arson and murder, convicted, and even put to death for a fire you did not set.

Fortunately today, there are scientific methods to investigate fires and determine actual causes. Instead of blaming the first person who escapes out of a burning house and building a criminal case around that victim's flawed character, modern-day investigators can rely on proven techniques, not arson folklore.

With gratitude, we recognize the work of the fire forensic experts who have revolutionized the manner in which fires are investigated today.

We honor those who have been victims of fires or wrongly convicted. Our hope is that they did not suffer in vain. Their criminal cases provided the catalyst for the evolution of fire science investigative techniques and conclusions. Because of their personal experiences and the knowledge that emerged, a paradigm shift occurred with our family's forty-year-old fire criminal case. It allowed suspicion, fear, and unresolved questions to be replaced by understanding, forgiveness, and relief. What were once indicators of arson were now proof that the fire was accidental in origin.

Perhaps the next time there is a house fire and a declaration of arson, it won't be simply accepted but fully investigated using modern-day fire forensic best practices.

I am deeply grateful for the many people who are part of my life and who traveled with me on this memory-dredging, storytelling, and book-writing journey. I started to investigate the fire with the help of Lt. Detective Chuck DeFebbo and Jim Barber, former

Brigantine City manager and former captain in charge of homicides for the Atlantic County Prosecutor's Office.

Their knowledge, dedication, and professionalism helped shape the course of my investigation. The Ventnor police and fire departments, as well as Brigantine police, were helpful in digging up ancient reports.

I began writing these memoirs in 2008. Several years later, in 2012, I enlisted the aid of a ghostwriter, Emily Adams, who wrote the first manuscript and co-authored the second manuscript. Without Emily's expertise, her keen investigative talents and relentless prodding to find answers, her commitment to the project, and her interaction with my sisters, this book would not have been written.

In 2015, once we finally obtained the truth about the fire from John DeHaan (a fellow truth seeker), my sister Lisa and I joined forces to finish the story. She was able to pick up where Emily left off, capture my voice, and put it into words. Lisa understood what I was trying to say.

Back in 1974, one of my sisters whispered to the world after the fire, "We're free," but little did they know how wrong they were then, because now, after forty years, we are truly free. We know that the fire wasn't arson and Lisa wasn't involved.

Today, I take pride in my accomplishments and my family. I remain thankful to Les, Lisa, and Liz for being my sisters and Jessica for being the best daughter ever. She inspires me and makes me laugh. I'm grateful to John and Betsy Rogge for their kindness, generosity, and love; Linda and Maurice Cole for their support and encouragement; and Doug and Jill Auburn, for trying to make it right when everything was going so wrong.

A special thanks and acknowledgement to the following:

Original Fire Investigation, 1974

Sergeant Gilbert	Ventnor Police Detective
William Rutley	Ventnor Deputy Fire Marshall

*Recent Fire Investigation,
2008–2016*

Kristine Bunch	Wrongfully convicted of arson in 1996, served seventeen years in Indiana prison
Fire Chief James Culbertson	Ventnor Fire Department
Dr. Gerald Hurst	American chemist and fire investigator
Gerald Wayne Lewis	Victim of Lime Street Fire 1990, charged with arson and eventually exonerated by modern forensic techniques
John Lentini	Expert Fire Forensic Investigator
Cameron Todd Willingham	Wrongfully convicted of arson, executed by the state of Texas on February 17, 2004

Friends and Family

San Ramon The Book Club	Readers of the early manuscript who provided feedback, insight, and support
Jim Cooper	Special friend who first proposed writing the story and never stopped believing
Linda Fetch and Tim Scott	Proofreaders, editors
Bud Lyons	Proofreader and longtime friend and mentor
Larissa Overton	Daughter of Lisa
Leah Overton Renshaw	Daughter of Leslie
Maria Overton	Daughter of Lisa
Patty McGuigan	Motivator and inspiration to writers everywhere
Bennett Wright	Proofreader and longtime friend
Susan Schulman	Literary Agent who provided invaluable guidance on publishing

APPENDIX

What to Do in Case of a Fire

Fires can happen to anyone, anytime, and anywhere without notice. According to the National Fire Protection Agency (NFPA), in 2016, there were 1,342,000 fires reported in the United States. These fires caused 3,390 civilian deaths, 14,650 civilian injuries, and $10.6 billion in property damage.

- 475,500 were structure fires, causing 2,950 civilian deaths, 12,775 civilian injuries, and $7.9 billion in property damage.
- 173,000 were vehicle fires, causing 280 civilian fire deaths, 1,075 civilian fire injuries, and $933 million in property damage.
- 662,500 were outside and other fires, causing 85 civilian fire deaths, 650 civilian fire injuries, and $1.4 billion in property damage.

Wildfires in 2017 that ripped through Northern California destroyed at least 8,400 homes and buildings, according to state officials with estimated total insured losses for the Northern California fires at $1.045 billion, based on preliminary figures by State Insurance Commissioner Dave Jones.

So how to survive? Your best chance of surviving a fire is to be prepared. You need to know the proper actions to take quickly. In a fire, seconds count, and lives and property can be saved.

Before you can take action, you need to understand that for fire to ignite, it needs three elements: heat, fuel, and oxygen. The process goes like this: Fuel or something combustible, like paper or cloth, is heated by an external source and gives off vapors. These vapors ignite and cause the chain reaction to begin that leads to a fire which can spread quickly burning everything in its path (source: Gulf News).

In just two minutes, a fire can become life-threatening. In five minutes, a residence can be engulfed in flames.

Learn about fires (source: https://www.ready.gov/home-fires).

- *Fire is* fast! In less than thirty seconds, a small flame can turn into a major fire. It only takes minutes for thick black smoke to fill a house or for a house to be engulfed in flames.
- *Fire is* hot! Heat is more threatening than flames. Room temperatures in a fire can be one hundred degrees at floor level and rise to six hundred degrees at eye level. Inhaling this superhot air will scorch your lungs and melt clothes to your skin. A fully developed room fire (called flashover) can grow from ignition in a modern upholstered sofa, chair, or mattress in three to five minutes in a bedroom or living room, at which time the temperatures can exceed one thousand degrees at both ceiling and floor, instantly fatal to an exposed human.
- *Fire is* dark! Fire starts bright, but quickly produces black smoke and complete darkness.
- *Fire is* deadly! Smoke and toxic gases kill more people than flames do. Fire produces poisonous gases that make you disoriented and drowsy. Asphyxiation is the leading cause of fire deaths, exceeding burns by a three-to-one ratio.

In Case of a Fire

- Set off the fire alarm or call 911.
- Warn people nearby to immediately evacuate the area.
- Close the door of the premises or area where the fire is located so as to contain it.

- Priority is to get yourself, family members, and co-workers out. *Do not* attempt to salvage equipment or objects—you are putting yourself at risk!

Remember

- If you are the last to leave the premises, close the doors to contain the fire, but do not lock them.
- Use the nearest stairs and exit, as long as it is free from smoke; otherwise, seek another evacuation route.
- Follow the instructions given over the PA system, if available.
- Do *not* use the elevators.
- If there is smoke, crawl out of the building or home.
- Do *not* stop at or near the exit. Leave the way free for other people evacuating the building.
- Go directly to the assembly point or a safe area.
- Do *not* reenter the evacuated building or home under any circumstances until you receive specific instructions to do so from the fire department.

In case you get stuck in a smoke-filled room when evacuating, remember to stay low. *You need to crawl on your hands and knees,* keeping your head in the safety zone (one to two feet above the floor). Cover your nose and mouth.

Most deaths in house or building fires are not due to burns but due to smoke inhalation. If you're able to find a handkerchief or towel, dip it in water and cover your nose. If you can't find one, take your shirt and cover your face up to just below your eyes. After that, stay low and crawl until you reach the exit.

When you see a closed door and you don't know if the other side is on fire, feel the door with the back of your hand. If it's hot, don't take that route if you can find another one.

If your shirt suddenly catches fire, don't panic. *Stop, drop,* and *roll* to snuff out the flames. Do not run as moving in air will fan the flames and spread them. Thin, loose-fitting fabrics are easily ignited.

Before opening a door, check if it is hot using *the back of your hand*. If the door feels hot, don't open the door. Also, if you see smoke under the door, you should not open the door. Otherwise, the toxic smoke and fire may enter the room and worsen the situation. If you are unable to open the door because of fire, try to escape through a window.

If the door feels cool, open it slow, look for smoke or flames, and pass through it, if clear.

Fire Prevention Essentials

1. Fire extinguisher
2. Fire blanket
3. Chain or collapsible ladder
4. Baking soda
5. Emergency bag

Before a Fire

Create and practice a fire escape plan.

In the event of a fire, remember that every second counts, so you and your family must always be prepared. Escape plans help you get out of your home quickly. No house is safe or resistant to a major fire if the room is fully exposed to a fully developed fire for more than a few minutes.

Twice each year, practice your home fire escape plan. Some tips to consider when preparing this plan include the following:

- Find two ways to get out of each room in the event the primary way is blocked by fire or smoke.
- A secondary route might be a window onto a neighboring roof or a collapsible ladder for escape from upper-story windows.
- Make sure that windows are not stuck, screens can be taken out quickly, and security bars can be properly opened.

- Practice feeling your way out of the house in the dark or with your eyes closed.
- Teach children not to hide from firefighters.

Smoke alarms.

A working smoke alarm significantly increases your chances of surviving a deadly home fire.

- Install both ionization *and* photoelectric smoke alarms, or dual-sensor smoke alarms, which contain both ionization and photoelectric smoke sensors.
- Test batteries monthly.
- Replace batteries in battery-powered and hardwired smoke alarms at least once a year (except non-replaceable ten-year lithium batteries).
- Install smoke alarms on every level of your home, including the basement, both inside and outside of sleeping areas.
- Replace the entire smoke alarm unit every eight to ten years or according to manufacturer's instructions.
- Never disable a smoke alarm while cooking—it can be a deadly mistake.

Smoke alarm safety for people with access or functional needs.

- Audible alarms for visually impaired people should pause with a small window of silence between each successive cycle so that they can listen to instructions or voices of others.
- Smoke alarms with a vibrating pad or flashing light are available for the hearing impaired. Contact your local fire department for information about obtaining a flashing or vibrating smoke alarm.
- Smoke alarms with a strobe light outside the home to catch the attention of neighbors and emergency call systems for summoning help are also available.

More Fire Safety Tips

Make digital copies of valuable documents and records like the following:

- Social Security cards
- Birth certificates
- Medical records
- Marriage records
- Passports
- Car and home titles
- Family photos or heirlooms

Keep these items in a single bag or binder that you can quickly grab on your way out of the home. Always keep in mind, however, that fires spread quickly and you may not be able to reach your valuables during an escape. For this reason, consider investing in a fireproof document storage device such as a home fire safe, many of which are capable to surviving fires of varying intensity. Check the fire rating on different storage devices to select the best one for you.

- Sleep with your door closed.
- Contact your local fire department for information on training on the proper use and maintenance of fire extinguishers.
- Consider installing an automatic fire sprinkler system in your residence.

Fire Escape Planning for Older Adults and People with Access or Functional Needs

- Live near an exit. You'll be safest on the ground floor if you live in an apartment building. If you live in a multistory home, arrange to sleep on the ground floor and near an exit.

- If you use a walker or wheelchair, check all exits to be sure you get through the doorways.
- Make any necessary accommodations, such as providing exit ramps and widening doorways, to facilitate an emergency escape.
- Speak to your family members, building manager, or neighbors about your fire safety plan and practice it with them.
- Contact your local fire department's nonemergency line and explain your special needs. Ask emergency providers to keep your special needs information on file.
- Keep a phone near your bed and be ready to call 911 or your local emergency number if a fire occurs.

After a Fire

The following checklist serves as a quick reference and guide for you to follow after a fire strikes.

- Contact your local disaster relief service, such as the Red Cross, if you need temporary housing, food, and medicines.
- If you are insured, contact your insurance company for detailed instructions on protecting the property, conducting inventory, and contacting fire damage restoration companies. If you are not insured, try contacting private organizations for aid and assistance.
- Check with the fire department to make sure your residence is safe to enter. Be watchful of any structural damage caused by the fire.
- The fire department should see that utilities are either safe to use or are disconnected before they leave the site. *Do not* attempt to reconnect utilities yourself.
- Conduct an inventory of damaged property and items. Do not throw away any damaged goods until after an inventory is made.

- Try to locate valuable documents and records. Refer to information on contacts and the replacement process inside this brochure.
- Begin saving receipts for any money you spend related to fire loss. The receipts may be needed later by the insurance company and for verifying losses claimed on income tax.
- Notify your mortgage company of the fire.

Prevent Home Fires

Home fires are preventable! The following are simple steps that each of us can take to prevent a tragedy.

Cooking

- Stay in the kitchen when you are frying, grilling, or broiling food. If you leave the kitchen for even a short period of time, turn off the stove.
- Wear short, close-fitting, or tightly rolled sleeves when cooking.
- Keep children away from cooking areas by enforcing a "kid-free zone" of three feet around the stove.
- Position barbecue grills at least ten feet away from siding and deck railings and out from under eaves and overhanging branches.

Smoking

- Smoke outside and completely stub out butts in an ashtray or a can filled with sand.
- Soak cigarette butts and ashes in water before throwing them away. Never toss hot cigarette butts or ashes in the trash can.
- Never smoke in a home where oxygen is used, even if it is turned off. Oxygen can be explosive and makes fire burn hotter and faster.

- Be alert—don't smoke in bed! If you are sleepy, have been drinking, or have taken medicine that makes you drowsy, put your cigarette out first.

Electrical and Appliance Safety

- Frayed wires can cause fires. Replace all worn, old, or damaged appliance cords immediately and do not run cords under rugs or furniture.
- If an appliance has a three-pronged plug, use it only in a three-slot outlet. Never force it to fit into a two-slot outlet or extension cord.
- Immediately shut off, and then professionally replace, light switches that are hot to the touch and lights that flicker.

Portable Space Heaters

- Keep combustible objects at least three feet away from portable heating devices.
- Buy only heaters evaluated by a nationally recognized laboratory, such as Underwriters Laboratories (UL).
- Check if the portable heater has a thermostat control mechanism and will switch off automatically if it falls over.
- Only use crystal-clear 1-K kerosene in kerosene heaters. Never overfill it. Use the heater in a well-ventilated room.
- Use the heater *only* in a well-ventilated room. Never add any gasoline to the fuel tank.
- Never use a charcoal grill inside at any time. The carbon monoxide it produces is lethal even at low concentrations.

Fireplaces and Woodstoves

- Inspect and clean woodstove pipes and chimneys annually and check monthly for damage or obstructions.

- Use a fireplace screen heavy enough to stop rolling logs and big enough to cover the entire opening of the fireplace to catch flying sparks.
- Make sure the fire is completely out before leaving the house or going to bed.
- Wood fire "coals" can remain hot for many hours after the flames have died. Coals may be cool to the touch but stay smoldering at the center. Place all coals and ashes in a sealed (covered) *metal* can outside and away from walls and shrubbery. Never place ashes or coals in a plastic household garbage can.

Children

- Take the mystery out of fire play by teaching children that fire is a tool, not a toy.
- Store matches and lighters out of children's reach and sight, preferably in a locked cabinet.
- Never leave children unattended near operating stoves or burning candles, even for a short time.

More Prevention Tips

- Never use stove range or oven to heat your home.
- Keep combustible and flammable liquids away from heat sources.
- Portable generators should *never* be used indoors and should only be refueled outdoors or in well-ventilated areas.
- When using any paint, stain, or varnish inside, read and follow all warnings on the container. Many such finishes today contain natural oils (linseed, tung nut, or others) that can self-heat, even at room temperature. After use, secure all wiping rags and drop cloths in a closed metal container filled with water away from the building.

Shareables

- *U.S. Fire Administration, www.usfa.fema.gov/prevention/ outreach*
- *Fire Prevention and Public Education, www.usfa.fema.gov/ prevention*
- *Outreach Materials and Educational Programs, www.usfa. fema.gov/prevention/outreach*
- *American Red Cross, www.redcross.org*
- *US Disaster Relief and Assistance, www.usa.gov/disaster-financial-help*
- *Salvation Army, www.salvationarmyusa.org*
- *United Way, www.unitedway.org*
- *Local charities, churches, and shelters*

ADDITIONAL RESOURCES

The following information is by no means comprehensive. Most of it is taken verbatim from the Internet. A specific need or geographical area can easily be targeted with the search engine of one's choice. Family, friends, and professional contacts are also a good source of aid and information.

Help for Fire Victims

- The *Red Cross* (www.redcross.org) can assist with immediate emergency disaster-caused needs including assistance with temporary lodging, food, clothing, replacement medications or eyewear, comfort kits with hygiene items, and storage containers for belongings. Red Cross mental health volunteers can support fire victims with grief and trauma counseling and referrals to local mental health care providers. Additional assistance the Red Cross can provide is first month's rent or security deposit and referrals to partner agencies for household goods, clothes, and other services.
- A nonprofit founded by the respected the Firefighters First Credit Union, *Fire Family Foundation* (https://firefamilyfoundation.org/about-us), offers immediate assistance to firefighters and their families, fire victims, fire departments, and charities. The foundation believes that by coming together as a "fire family," assistance can be provided to those impacted by fire.
- The *Disaster Assistance Improvement Program* (https://www.disasterassistance.gov/) will provide disaster survivors with information, support, services, and a means to access and apply for disaster assistance through joint data-shar-

ing efforts between federal, tribal, state, local, and private sector partners. Although this website is for widespread, government-declared disasters, there are many resources linked to this site.

Housing and Homeless Services

- The *Salvation Army* (http://www.salvationarmyusa.org/) has group homes, emergency shelters, and transitional living centers that provide housing, food, and overnight lodging for varying amounts of time to those in need. In addition, they provide educational, counseling, and vocational services to homeless, destitute individuals and families and youth where family care is undesirable or unavailable. For those families with temporal needs, family service programs help families and needy individuals with emergency food, housing, and utility assistance.

Resources for the Unjustly Accused

- The *Innocence Project* (http://www.innocenceproject.org/) founded in 1992 by Barry Scheck and Peter Neufeld is a national litigation and public policy organization dedicated to exonerating wrongfully convicted individuals through DNA testing and reforming the criminal justice system to prevent future injustice. The Innocence Project's mission is to free the staggering number of innocent people who remain incarcerated and to bring reform to the system responsible for their unjust imprisonment.
- The Innocence Project in California: https://californiainnocenceproject.org/issues-we-face/fire-investigation/.
- *Wrongful Conviction and Innocence Resources on the Internet*: http://www.llrx.com/features/wrongfulconviction.htm#innocence. Many people have been falsely accused and wrongly convicted in our criminal justice system. This site contains a bibliography which focuses on the key web-

sites and resources concerning this important issue. Dozens of resources are linked here.

- *The National Registry of Exonerations*: http://www.law. umich.edu/special/exoneration/Pages/about.aspx.
- The **Victims of Crime Resource Center** is located on the Pacific McGeorge School of Law campus in Sacramento, California (http://1800victims.org/crime-type/arson). The center has operated the state of California's confidential, toll-free **1-800-VICTIMS** line since 1984.
- *interFire Online* (http://www.interfire.org/resourcecenter. asp) has a compilation of documents, tools, abstracts, and references to help explore specific fire and fire investigation topics. Every month, a new addition covers a wealth of fire investigation information ranging from preliminary fire scene assessments to fire insurance fraud.
- *Online Science Degree* (http://onlinefiresciencedegree.org/ fire-investigation/) is an educational site which also provides resources for students and others, including links to more than eighty national and regional organizations, as well as private firms, explosion investigation resources, fire investigation attorneys, and additional sites and organizations.
- *Bluhm Legal Clinic Center on Wrongful Convictions*: http:// www.law.northwestern.edu/legalclinic/wrongfulconvictions/exonerations/in/kristine-bunch.html.

Additional Articles of Interest

- PBS interview with Gerald Hurst: http://www.pbs. org/wgbh/pages/frontline/death-by-fire/interviews/gerald-hurst.html
- The Beyler report about Cameron Todd Willingham: http://alt.coxnewsweb.com/shared-blogs/austin/investigative/upload/2009/08/execution_based_on_bad_investi/D_Beyler%20FINAL%20REPORT%20082509. pdf

ABOUT THE AUTHOR

Leigh Overton Boyd is the oldest of four sisters to survive a house fire outside of Atlantic City in June 1974 that killed her parents. In the years following the fire investigation, Leigh earned a degree in criminal justice, studied the law, and became Miss Atlantic City. The mother of two children, one of whom she lost to muscular dystrophy, she has a successful real estate consulting business in the San Francisco Bay Area. Recently, Leigh moved to Idaho to be with her lifelong partner, golden retriever therapy dog and hunting dog, and two Balinese cats. This is her first book.